Anthony Pasquin

The New Brighton Guide

Involving a complete authentic, and honorable solution of the recent

mysteries of Carlton house

Anthony Pasquin

The New Brighton Guide
Involving a complete authentic, and honorable solution of the recent mysteries of Carlton house

ISBN/EAN: 9783337152383

Printed in Europe, USA, Canada, Australia, Japan

Cover: Foto ©Andreas Hilbeck / pixelio.de

More available books at **www.hansebooks.com**

THE

NEW BRIGHTON GUIDE.

Price Two Shillings.

𝕰𝖓𝖙𝖊𝖗𝖊𝖉 𝖆𝖙 𝕾𝖙𝖆𝖙𝖎𝖔𝖓𝖊𝖗𝖘' 𝕳𝖆𝖑𝖑.

THE

NEW BRIGHTON GUIDE;

INVOLVING A

COMPLETE, AUTHENTIC, AND HONORABLE

SOLUTION

OF THE

RECENT MYSTERIES

OF

CARLTON HOUSE,

By *ANTHONY PASQUIN*, Esq.

THE SIXTH EDITION:
WITH MOMENTOUS ALTERATIONS AND ADDITIONS.

Qui ambulat simpliciter, ambulat confidenter; et qui depravat vias suas manifestus erit.

LONDON:

PRINTED FOR H. D. SYMONDS, PATERNOSTER ROW; AND
T. BELLAMY, KING STREET, COVENT GARDEN.

1796.

THE

NEW BRIGHTON GUIDE.

A MORAL EPISTLE

FROM

THE PAVILION AT BRIGHTON *

TO

CARLTON HOUSE, LONDON.

DEAR COUSIN CARLEY,

It was said, and said wisely, that telling one's grief,
In a certain degree, will insure us relief:
And I hope you're too just, though I'm craz'd and forlorn,
To unite with the vulgar, and treat me with scorn.
That I'm not what I was, is but wofully true;
But I trust I shall ever be valu'd by you.
Ah me! what a change has occurr'd in my state,
Since HE who enjoy'd me has prov'd an ingrate!

I am

---

* BRIGHTHELMSTONE, or BRIGHTON, in Sussex, is 54 miles from London.
—It was, like Amsterdam, a miserable-fishing town, but is now a place of importance; to which it was raised by the countenance and bounty of the PRINCE of WALES. The houses are, generally speaking, more inconvenient than unhandsome; and the streets are narrow and irregular. In the year 1699, more than 100 huts were swallowed by the sea; and in a few years more, all the tenements on the Cliffs will be similarly devoured, unless a very formidable embankment is erected to resist that imperious element.——It is one of those numerous watering-places which beskirt this polluted island, and operate as apologies for idleness, sensuality, and nearly all the ramifications of social imposture: where the barren seek a stimulus for fecundity; the

THE

NEW BRIGHTON GUIDE.

A MORAL EPISTLE

FROM

*THE PAVILION AT BRIGHTON**

TO

CARLTON HOUSE, LONDON.

DEAR COUSIN CARLEY,

It was said, and said wisely, that telling one's grief,
In a certain degree, will insure us relief:
And I hope you're too just, though I'm craz'd and forlorn,
To unite with the vulgar, and treat me with scorn.
That I'm not what I was, is but wofully true;
But I trust I shall ever be valu'd by you.
Ah me! what a change has occurr'd in my state,
Since HE who enjoy'd me has prov'd an ingrate!

I am

---

* BRIGHTHELMSTONE, or BRIGHTON, in Sussex, is 54 miles from London. —It was, like Amsterdam, a miserable-fishing town, but is now a place of importance, to which it was raised by the countenance and bounty of the PRINCE of WALES. The houses are, generally speaking, more inconvenient than unhandsome; and the streets are narrow and irregular. In the year 1699, more than 130 huts were swallowed by the sea; and in a few years more, all the tenements on the Cliffs will be similarly devoured, unless a very formidable embankment is erected to resist that imperious element.——It is one of those numerous watering-places which beskirt this polluted island, and operate as apologies for idleness, sensuality, and nearly all the ramifications of social imposture: where the barren seek a stimulus for fecundity; the

volup-

I am like an old wife, now, continually weeping—

Who would think, from my visage, I e'er was in keeping?

When he first nestled here he was handsome and thin,

No razor had then mown his stubbleless chin:

He was sportive and careless, bland, upright, and young,

And I smil'd on his feats when he said or he sung:

Then

voluptuary to wash the cobwebs from the interstices of his flaccid anatomy; and the swag-bellied denizen, the rancid adhesion of old cheese, Irish butter, junk, assa-fœtida, tallow, mundungus, and train-oil.——There are two taverns, namely, the Castle and the Old Ship, where the richer visitors resort; and at each of these houses a weekly assembly is held, where a master of the ceremonies attends, to arrange the parties, not according to the scale of utility, but that of aristocracy.——There is a ball every Monday at the Castle, and on Thursdays at the Old Ship: every subscriber pays three shillings and sixpence, and every non-subscriber five shillings; for which they are entitled to a beverage which they call *tea* and *coffee*.—— The masters of the respective inns receive the profits, except on those nights appointed for the benefit of the master of the ceremonies; to whom all, who wish to be arranged as people of distinction, subscribe one guinea— and who would not purchase distinction at so cheap a rate? Independently of this vain *douceur*, they must pay most liberally for their tickets! The card assemblies are on Wednesdays and Fridays.—There is an hotel, which was intended as a country Hummums, or grand dormitory; but, in my weak opinion, the establishment is somewhat inefficient, unless it can be supposed that the tumultuous equipment of stage-coaches, at the dawn of day, is contributory to the purposes of rest.——There is a theatre, commodious, and generally well directed; the nights of performance are Tuesdays and Wednesdays, Fridays and Saturdays. At the lower end of North-street is a sort of Birmingham Vauxhall, called the *Promenade Grove*: it is a small inclosure of a paddock, tormented from its native simplicity, befringed with a few gawkey poplars, and decorated with flowers, bowers, benches, frogs, ground-ivy, a ditch, and a wooden box for the minstrels. ——The coast is like the greater part of its visitors, bold, saucy, intrusive, and dangerous.——The bathing-machines, even for the ladies, have no awning or covering, as at Weymouth, Margate, and Scarborough; consequently they are all severely inspected by the aid of telescopes, not only as they confusedly ascend from the sea, but as they kick and sprawl and flounder about its muddy margin, like so many mad Naiads in flannel

smocks:

Then youth bore its own pardon, while stumbling o'er ill,

As the passions o'erthrew what was meant by the will.

When the full ardent Moon, from her silvery post,

O'erheated the sculls of the world's motley host;

Made the chymist more zealous to transmute his dross,

And adventurers losing to treble that loss;

I have

smocks:—the shore is so disastrously imperfect, that those beginners who paddle in, are injured by the shocking repulsion of the juices to the brain; and of those who are enabled to plunge in, and swim beyond the surge, it is somewhat less than an even bet that many never return—in truth, the loss of lives here every season, would make any society miserable, who were not congregating in the mart of noisy folly ——There is a Subscription House, or Temple of Fortune, on the Steyne, where the minor part of our blessed nobility are accustomed to reduce their characters and their estates in the same period;—the signal for admittance is *habeo*—for rejection, *debeo.*——There are lodgings of all descriptions and fitness, from twenty pounds per week on the Cliffs, to half a crown per night in a stable; and the sinews of morality are so happily relaxed, that a bawd and a baroness may snore in the same tenement;—the keepers of the lodging-houses, like the keepers of mad-houses, having but one common point in view—to *bleed* the parties sufficiently.——There are carriages and caravans of all shapes and dimensions, from a waggon to a fish-cart; in which you may move like a king, a criminal, or a crab, that is, forwards, backwards, or laterally ——There are two libraries on the Steyne, replete with every flimsy species of novels, involving the prodigious intrigues of an imaginary society: this kind of recreation is termed *light reading;* perhaps from the certain effect it has upon the brains of my young countrywomen, of making them *light-headed!*——There is a parish church, where the *canaill* go to pray; but as that is on a hill, and the gentry found their sabbath visit to the Almighty very troublesome, the amiable and accommodating *master* priest has consigned the care of his common *parish mutton* to his *journeyman,* the curate, and has kindly raised a Chapel Royal for the *lambs of fashion,* where a certain sum is paid for every seat: and this, it must be admitted, is as it should be; as a well-bred deity will assuredly be more attentive to a reclining Dutchess, parrying the assaults of the devil behind her fan, than the vulgar piety of a plebeian on his knees. —— There were books open in the circulating libraries, where you were requested to contribute your mite of charity to the support of the rector, as his income is some-

B 2

what

I have seen him inwove with a pestilent crew,

Who nine-tenths came undone, and the rest to undo!

When those caitiffs came thund'ring in impudent state,

And drew up their *tandems* and *gigs* at my gate,

Full of wrath at their daring, I rav'd and I swore,

Then I let in an Eddy that slamm'd to the door :

But, alas ! it avail'd not—'twas open'd again,

And the P—— rose, and welcom'd the toad-eating train !

He urbane smil'd on all, where 'twas sin to look sad,

As God's light aids in common the good and the bad.

I tore off Folly's cloak to exhibit the wrong ;

How I toil'd to advise, but was stunn'd with a song :

I made signs on my plaster to rally them all,

But no *Daniel* was there to decipher the wall.——

Ah ! I know his large heart and beneficent plan ;

Though he's run from the course, yet HE FEELS LIKE A MAN ·

Though he dissipates seeds of an undeserv'd sorrow,

And gaily puts off half his ills till the morrow,

His radical nobleness knows no decay ;

He will act, but not cant—he'll relieve ere he'll pray :

As Charity's retinue own, while embrac'd,

IN HIS GIFT HE GIVES TWICE, 'TIS A DEED SO WELL GRAC'D.

what less than seven hundred pounds a year; the last incumbent died worth thirty thousand pounds. During the first dawnings of convalescence after the suspension of the King's intellectual faculties, he asked Dr. WILLIS how much he netted by his Lincolnshire pluralities—"Eight hundred per year," was the reply.--"Then why," added the monarch, "do you, who are so rich, undertake to cure mad people for hire ?"—"I imitate Jesus Christ, sire, who went about doing good."—"Yes ; but," rejoined his Majesty, " in the first place, Jesus Christ did good for nothing ; and in the second, he had not eight hundred a year, my friend !"

When

When their mirth grew to madness, and jests met the
    ear,
Which Philosophy scorns, and no maiden should hear,
Convuls'd with disdain I soon alter'd their note,
For I shut up the principal valve of my throat;
Till the smoke in vast volumes pour'd into their room,
And enwrapp'd the loud mob in a horrible gloom,
More fœtid than Vulcan inhal'd with his breath;
More thick than e'er pass'd o'er the threshold of Death;
More choking than Cyclops drank in at their forge;
More rank than the reptile of Thebes could disgorge:
As they gasp'd, it rush'd down their intestines, and clogg'd
    'em,
And from *pharynx* to *rectum* begrim'd and befogg'd 'em:
While hoarsely they growl'd at the house and the smother,
Though, by knowing the cause, they had curs'd one another.
'Mid their baneful carousals I've fum'd and I've fretted,
Till from kitchen to garret I've croak'd and I've sweated;
By pressure I made my joints crack—I can't bawl—
And drops, drawn from my heart, ran from every wall:
But his H———ss, not knowing my woes or displeasure,
Renew'd the broad catch, and refill'd every measure;
While the rascals around him, revil'd the damp mansion,
And my marrow scorch'd up by the fire's expansion:
Which so heated my fibres and bones—I mean wood—
That a putrescent fever polluted my blood;
Which settled behind the bed's-head of the P———e,
And I've not had my health or my ease ever since;

                                  Yet

Yet I'm sure he would grieve, his politeness is such,
Had he known that a lady had suffer'd so much.
Thus they swill'd and reswill'd, and repeated their boozings,
Till their shirts became dy'd with purpureal oozings.
When the *taster* sought wine of a primary sort,
I have cough'd 'neath the bin, and shook all the old port,
Till 'twas muddy as WILL B—CK's brains—yet each varlet
Said 'twas bright as a ruby, and toasting some harlot,
Would then smack his lips in despite of my labor !
Oh ye gods ! how I wish'd for a fist and a sabre,
To cut down the hiccupping braggarts with glee,
That is, if their heads could be injur'd by me.
When WELTJIE has cook'd for the half-famish'd group,
How oft have I belch'd pecks of soot in his soup :
Yet e'en that could not drive them from board or from bed,
Though 'twas render'd as black as an Ethiop's head :
When I've made it as foul as a Scot's ragged tartan,
The rogues gulp'd it down, and all swore it was Spartan.
When they've sat near the fire in knee-squeezing rows,
I have spit out a coal, and demolish'd their hose :
All my grates have breath'd sulphur to stifle their powers ;
I'd a watch in my sides to beat minutes and hours :
When I've seen a Blight glide 'twixt the earth and the skies,
I've coax'd in the demon, and ruin'd their eyes :
I have edg'd down a poker on legs swell'd with gout,
Till the miscreant has roar'd like swine stuck in the snout :
When Lord ——— from my windows was making a beck,
I have hurl'd down my sashes, and wounded his neck ;

Though

Though my rage could but bruise him black, yellow, and
 blue,
'Twas a hint that might show what the nation should do :
But each knave all the arts of my anger withstood,
For the leeches will suck while the body has blood.
I'd have prophesied much, had I Cerberus' three tongues ;
I would fulminate oaths, but, alas ! I've no lungs.
When they thought 'twas an earthquake that palsied my
 walls,
It was I who was shuddering to witness their brawls.
There's no office so dirty but they would fulfil ;
There's no sense of debasement could alter their will :
When the munching of immature codlings might gripe
 him,
They would tear out the leaves of the Psalter to wipe
 him.
Yet these summer-fed vermin will fly him, if e'er
His wintery fortunes should leave his trunk bare ;
Then he'll know that but virtue can keep the soul great,
As they'd make their past meanness the *cause* of their hate !
I have dropp'd lumps of lime in their glasses while drinking ;
I've made thieves in the candle to move him to thinking ;
I have clatter'd my casements and chairs to confound 'em ;
I have let in the dews and the blast all around 'em ;
I have elbow'd my timbers 'gainst many a head ;
I have stirr'd up the sewers to stink 'em to bed :
Yet this mass of antipathy marr'd my own liver,
And my tears fill'd the gutter like Egypt's deep river.

      —My

—My eyes, my dear Coz, are exhausted with crying ;
So I'll give o'er at present--I'm yours till I'm dying.

    Steyne, Brighthelmstone,   PAVILION.
      August 6th, 1796.

P. S. My respects to *old* JAMES. When I write by next post,⎤
   I will send you an *Ode,* which this bacchanal host   ⎬
   Sung or said, and alarm'd all the fish from our coast. ⎦

A

SENTIMENTAL EPISTLE

FROM

CARLTON HOUSE

TO

THE PAVILION AT BRIGHTON.

MY DEAR LITTLE PAV.

PR'YTHEE whence could you get so much gall for your pen?
But let me set you right, who've more knowledge of men :
You evince to possess an illustrious soul—
You are right in the abstract, but wrong in the whole.
That his H———ss's rev'llers you treat with disdain,
I approve ; but let Charity marshal your vein ;
As I've not yet resolv'd, but he's less safe, by half,
With the knaves who seem grave, than with varlets who
    laugh.

                                  In

In the love of our lives we forget what we owe;
For the heart runs in debt, while the passions bestow :
As the latter, like truants, when vicious, will run,
And make the heart answer that mischief they'd done.—
Now the broad robe of manhood is wove for his shoulders ;
Now he stands as a mark for the region's beholders;
Mean Policy now supersedes his lov'd Truth,
And that permit's destroy'd which was granted his youth :
No excuse, like a *courier avant*, scuds before him,
No apologist waits to repurge and restore him.
That oblivion is past, which the liberal meant
Should envelope the fact, and but show the intent :
P*** has stripp'd him quite naked, and burnt ev'ry cover,
Where his frailties could hide, or as husband or lover ;
And left him expos'd to the blast and the beam,
The frost of repugnance, and sycophant's gleam ;
With domestics call'd forth from the haunts of his foes,
Whom he cannot approve, and he will not oppose :
As *one wily* ****, to eschew his disgrace,
Spunge up all he yields, but to squeeze o'er their race ;
By dread incantations, to calumny dear,
With *a tale of a tub* + cheat the popular ear ;

Act

+ Some few months since, the public mind was agitated with dire
alarms, engendered and supported by the most malignant subtlety; a
certain lady was tied to the stake, and baited by the mini-terial journal-
ists with the fury of cannibals.—The odious tale was circulated with every
struggle of bitterness, from one extremity of the realm to the other; every
one laboured to appear outrageously moral, by an effort to destroy the
marked sacrifice ; and it was a circumstance of peril, to question the
justice, the decency, and the authenticity or loyalty of their proceedings.
After an awful interim of suspension, it forsooth appeared, that a wander-

c

ing

Act up to the little designs of their chief,

Till that phantom, Morality, bleeds in belief;

And a lady's destroy'd by their fibs and their funning,

Whose only defect was, a want of—*their cunning!*

While he play'd on the waters of life without care,

Independent of guile, and unknown to despair;

Haply splashing what pass'd, without meaning offence,

The gay victim of Hazard, the minion of Sense;

Often doing that deed which Discretion would shun,

High above all disguise, and as bland as the sun;

He was gull'd down the stream, where the breakers destroy,

And the whirlpool's fell circles ingulph'd all his joy:

Thus he'll run and re-run, giddy, helpless, and light,

Till his spirit's absorb'd in indefinite night!—

He was promis'd God wot—Fortunatus's cap;—

Indemnity—duplicates—jewels— * * * *

* * * * * * * * * * * * *

* * * * * * * * * * * * *

ing priest had received a bundle of letters from an illustrious lady to carry with him abroad; but his wife becoming tormented with the tooth-ache, he declined the expedition; and returned the magic packet, which, it seems, was never received; yet, on this sandy basis, was the honor of a lady most vindictively overthrown, and the heir-apparent of a kingdom most scandalously insulted; and what adds to the mischievous mystery is, that all this was perpetrated by men who *affect* to have the good and dignity of the monarchy at heart, although such ruinous and insidious conduct operated to shake the regal pedestal more than all the efforts of all the *professed* republicans! Among the many extraordinary events to which this dark deed of crooked policy has given birth, may be noted the apt intervention of Lord T———, who volunteered it on this serio-comic occasion, to prove the absolute necessity of preserving a chaste deportment in life, and the danger of eternal perdition to those who lived in the beastly habits of adultery!

Was it done ?—do not ask—count your beads, and go pray ;
For *mum* is the order which governs the day.

They caught him while melting with Love's lambent
 flame,
In the blaze of affection—the acme of fame ;
They seiz'd him, while warm, in the precincts of beauty,
And sous'd him all o'er in the cold baths of duty.
Ere that lineament's faded which govern'd his sigh—
Ere that tablet's remov'd which impress'd the soul's eye—
Ere that odour had perish'd which freighted her kiss—
Ere the fibre ceas'd thrilling with Sympathy's bliss—
Ere the birth of new wonders had lessen'd his care—
As the system was writhing, and touch'd by despair ;
They bisected that nerve whence his hope knew increase,
And the web was unravell'd that shelter'd his peace.
Like a fen-gather'd vapour, or insect-fraught wind,
THEY MILDEW'D A HARVEST THAT GLADDEN'D MANKIND !
Who can say what would be in a crisis so try'd ?
Who can answer for ends when the means are deny'd ?
Though the nymph were more charmful than *Zeuxis* e'er
 saw—
Though the nation demanded the deed as a law—
Though *heralds* proclaim'd her august, as they do—
Though her manners were perfect, her sentiment true—
Though she rose, like Aurora, by zephyrs new fann'd—
Though she came, like young Spring, breathing health to
 the land—

      Though

Though she burst, like Jove's Hebe, transcendently bright—
Though blithe as the first emanation of light—
Though temper'd in thought by sweet Chastity's fire—
Though each Grace hail'd her step, and each God her desire:
Yet e'en such may not primary habits destroy,
Or compel the slow pulses to quicken in joy:
As who can act up to a passion that's feign'd?
The heart's noblest energies cannot be chain'd.

　To return to yourself, my dear PAV.*, you but prove
How inconstant we are e'en to that which we love:
I remember the time when you bragg'd of your downs,
Your salubrious breezes, wheat-ears, and green-gowns;
Your mackerel, that leap'd from the sea to the pot;
Your flat-fish and maids, and your soles, and what not;
Your fine views of the billows that roar round our isle;
Your large draughts of salt water to drench out the bile;
Your mirth at the fellows who p—'d 'gainst your rails;
Your licentious embraces with amorous Gales;
Your inns, where the bills won't admit of your sotting;
Your church-yards, where bodies have pleasure in rotting;

---

　* The Pavilion is built principally of wood: it is a nondescript monster in building, and appears like a mad-house, or a house run mad, as it has
neither beginning, middle, nor end; yet to acquire this design, a miserable
bricklayer was dispatched to Italy, to gather something equal to the required magnificence, and actually charged two thousand guineas for his
expenses.—There are four pillars in *scagliola*, in a sort of an oven, where the
Prince dines; and when the fire is lighted, the room is so hot, that the
parties are nearly baked and incrusted. The ground on which it is erected
was given to the Prince by the town, for which he allows them fifty pounds
yearly, to purchase grog and tobacco; and has so far mended their ways, as
to make a common sewer to hold all the current filth of the parish.

Your

Your machines, where the pennyless get lodging gratis ;

Your priest, who, each night, tells the gamesters how late
 'tis ;

Your flocks, rich as Tempe's, on each hillock grazing ;

And fifty more points as well sketch'd and amazing :

Yet now you're, forsooth, calling out to be pitied,

'Cause you've had too much faith, and have been too self-
 witted !—

I protest I'm so anger'd you've turn'd such a fool,

Were you but some years younger, I'd send you to school :

But learn this from an elder, all things are revolving,

And one prejudice sinks in another dissolving :

When our wish becomes realiz'd, Rapture foregoes

That estate in our mind whence she parried our woes ;

In having, we lose half we priz'd in the toy ;

In commanding a blessing, we narrow our joy.

Hope at best is a strumpet, who smiles to betray,

Who'll deny the next morn what she promis'd to-day :

She holds seeming cordials to interest our lips,

But embitters the draught while the simpleton sips :

Her influence, like fire, dispelling cold glooms,

Eternally warms, but in warming consumes :

There are few would be grappling at what they exact,

Would the gypsey Cumæan develope the fact.

<table>
<tr><td>Pall Mall,</td><td>Yours, as in duty bound,</td></tr>
<tr><td>August 8d, 1796.</td><td></td></tr>
<tr><td></td><td>CARLTON HOUSE.</td></tr>
</table>

ANOTHER MORAL EPISTLE

FROM

THE PAVILION AT BRIGHTON

TO

CARLTON HOUSE.

MY DEAR CARLEY,

'Tis a saying, as ancient as Greece, that none know

In what manner the pantoufle pinches the toe,

But the object who wears it : yet you, in a strain

Of indecorous heat, bid me cease to complain :

All this may be vastly in point, not to fret ;

But believe me I'm not so philosophis'd yet.

As to grinning when jobbernowls urin'd upon me,

'Tis false, by my honor :—who d'ye think has undone me?

There's MARLBOROUGH HOUSE knows, the last time they

did it,

I preach'd them a sermon * to check and forbid it ;

And now e'en the sauciest decently hie

In corners remote from the general eye.

---

* The insulted and injured lady, it is evident, borrowed her text on this singular occasion from SAMUEL, where the injunction is wonderfully appropriate to all the purposes of her decent wrath;—it runs thus : " If I leave of all that pertain to him that pisseth against the wall;" and she must have been inspired on this momentous occasion, as she was never known to be articulate before or since.

Had

Had I BANGOR's huge fist, I'd have pummell'd the scroyles;
But it's best as it is, as I execrate broils.
I've the *tedium vitæ, ennui,* and look blue;
I've ta'en bark, and *liqueurs,* and a dram—but 'twon't do.
I could moralize now till the sun left the west,
Till the night cools my lawn, or pale *Hecate's* undrest.
In a round of enjoyments, my exquisite friend,
Believe me there's neither beginning nor end:
'Tis pursuing a shadow that makes the soul sad,
And, like dogs in a circle, we run ourselves mad:
They enfeeble the mind like a lunatic's dreams,
As our joys, like our beauties, are prov'd by extremes;
Yet the bliss is short-liv'd with the drab or the sot,
As no pleasure remains where the virtues are not.

Whate'er your opinion of rustics may be,
We have *Rules for Good Breeding* *, and those you shall see.

I have

* TWELVE GOLDEN RULES *for young Gentlemen of Distinction, to be observed at Brighton for the Year* 1796.

First—Young and inexperienced officers must confederate with several of their mess as young as themselves, and reel into the theatre during the performance in a state of assumed intoxication, and be sure to disturb the audience in the most interesting part of the drama, by taking liberties with any of those Cyprian nymphs who harbour in the green boxes, and are unhappily devoted to insult: by this manœuvre, if dexterously managed, they will gain three important points;—the first is, the credit of having con-umed more wine than their income will allow; the second is, a disposition for unlimited intrigue; and the third is, an opportunity of displaying their contempt of good manners without any hazard of personal danger.—This behaviour will be totally out of character if any of the parties have seen service, or arrived at the years of discretion.

N. B. All descendants or members of the tribes of Israel, must neither mention lottery tickets, *omnium, loans,* scrip, navy, nor exchequer bills: they
must

I have sent you a copy along with *the Oat*,

Which I've charg'd BOULTON's lads not to lose on the road.

This

must pay their tradesmen on Saturdays, laugh at the paschal, eat swine, and shave every day.

Secondly—It is necessary at the assembly to make their homage to the *arbiter deliciarum, dragon rouge*, or master of the ceremonies, square with their local condition; as a trader or curate must nearly prostrate himself, to gain those civilities which a peer can command, by an inclination of that part of his anatomy which *he* calls a head.

Thirdly—All persons who are conscious of their insufficiency in personal merit, must seize every possible opportunity of prating and vaunting about their antiquity of blood and magnificence of consanguinity; and whether the account be true or otherwise, the attempt is justifiable, as those who have not dignity to support their own reputations should assuredly rely upon those who have.

Fourthly—The conduct of all, during the race week, should be systematic; and those who can keep coaches, phaetons, curricles, tandems, desobligeants, buggies, gigs, geldings, or taxed carts, have a privilege to murder all those pedestrians who cannot— as it is the saturnalia of Folly, he who gets to the goal first is unquestionably the best man. When on the course, it is supremely vulgar to be suspected of seeing three yards without a glass. As they pass the Prince, it will be *stylish* to salute him with an air of familiarity, which he will respectfully return, as his affability was never doubted; by this incident the buckeens from the city may be enabled to *cut a swell* with their associates, and appear the intimates of the Heir-Apparent, without the presumed requisites of wisdom, morality, erudition, or honor.

Fifthly—As there are no prescribed and marked roads in the purlieus of Brighton, or on the downs, for the jockey or the charioteer, they may indulge themselves in riding over an old woman, a walking philosopher, or a *trading quiz*, with impunity; and if the unfortunate scoundrel should die, a *genteel* jury may not only cover their lives, but protect them even from the inconveniences of a *dedland:* if, on examining the corpse of the *bourgeois*, it should prove to have been a creditor of the party, it will make the frolic immortal.

Sixthly— All pensioners at the boarding-houses must approach the head of the table by seniority. A considerable forfeit must be imposed if one gentleman cuts another's fingers in the avidity of carving for himself. No one to commence a discourse on politics or religion, but under the penalty of a pot of coffee. All blunders to be explained by the president

of

This place is so chang'd, from its manners and mirth,
That I scarce can believe 'tis the spot gave me birth :

Half

of the *table d'hote*, unless they come from an Irishman, who is permitted
to speak twice : and that person must be ignominiously expelled from the
establishment who is caught in the act of pocketting the fruit. If any take
an emetic to eat again, they shall suffer death without the *benefit* of
clergy.

Seventhly—If any are known to take pride in the ignoble science of
carving, *id est*, to *unbrace* a duck, *rear* a goose, *wing* a partridge, *thigh* a
woodcock, *allay* a pheasant, *rump* a pigeon, *unlace* a rabbit, *reduce* a chicken,
elevate a capon, *unjoint* a bustard, *display* a lark, *dissect* an ortolan, or *dis-
member* an heron, they shall be compelled to help the company before they
eat any themselves.

N. B. It is necessary to observe, that the ladies must be accommodated first.

Eighthly—All persons who sleep, sojourn, or masticate, at the Hotel,
Castle or Ship Taverns, must take especial care to make the profits of the
waiters greater than those of their masters ; which, it must be admitted, is
no easy matter : the reason for this apparently prodigal measure is, that all
importance at watering-places is *reflected*, and he to whom the waiters are
most obedient, is considered as the greater personage.

N. B. This rule does not extend to those who never pay their bills at sight.

Ninthly—In the mode of communicating their desires, they must punctu-
ally adhere to the following progressive statement :—if a Duke, he must
address that portion of the community, whom it is habitual to call *his* infe-
riors, by the style and title of *honest man*, or *honest woman* ; if a Marquis,
Earl, Viscount, Baron, or Bishop, by the unornamented term of *man* or
woman ; if a Baronet, Knight, Civilian, Physician, or any of that multi-
tudinous order which are denominated *small gentry*, they must use the plain
epithet *friend* ; but this must be marked by a strong emphasis, and accompanied with a certain talismanic and disdainful toss of the head, lest the poor
credulous devils might imagine the parties were sincere.

N. B. This rule must be equally and pertinaciously observed by the several
gradations of ladies correspondent with the gentlemen.

Tenthly—All must know, that the keeper of a boarding-house has the following rights :—if a *two-pounder*, or *gourmand*, should happen to mingle in
the circle, the purveyor may endeavour to get rid of him by persuading him
that the air is too sharp for his lungs; if that mode fails, the chambermaid
is ordered to leave his bed unmade, take away the *commodité*, damp the
sheets, and hide his night-cap; if that expedient is passed over, he is sent
to Coventry ; and if that is unpropitious, he is openly denied a chair, a

D   plate,

Half the houses are lanterns, much brick and much glass ;
Half the ladies are tinder ; the men lead or brass.

'Tis

plate, a knife, a fork, and a welcome ; and if that is unsuccessful, he is
advertised, described, and pounded as a stray cormorant, who will be sent
to his parish upon paying the expenses.

Eleventhly—All who are married, must exhibit a public contempt for their
wives in proportion to their rank in life, or what is termed quality ; as it
would be a species of petty treason for a trader to be as negligent of the
legal partner of his bed as a patrician, who, in various instances, may be
considered as elevated far above duty, thought, and character. None, of any
condition superior to the *mob*, must exhibit symptoms of conjugal fondness, as
that would imply a privation of taste and sentiment : whenever the names
of their wives occur in dialogue, they must affect deafness, to avoid a partici-
pation in the colloquy, as a declaration of any interest in their favor might
excite the wonder of the *beau monde*, and the sneers of their *cicisbei*.

Twelfthly—All bachelors must consider the spinsters as their destined
prey ; and if they cannot enjoy their persons, they may make free with
their reputations, which is nearly an universal case.—If they would be considered as fellows of spirit, they must signify, by some irregular gesticulation, that they have been well with every celebrated impure, or demirep,
who is existing, or has existed in their time : but this capital manœuvre
must not be carried beyond an insinuation, as, should they swear to the
event, there are none will believe them. When walking in the Assembly,
Grove, Steyne, or sitting at the Prince's Chapel (for it is supremely vulgar
to be seen at the parish church), they must occasionally nod at the most
dignified woman, the first fortune, or the greatest beauty, in the circle ; as
that will give them an undescribable air of fashion and *ton* : but they
must take especial care to do it while the parties are looking in another
direction, as otherwise their responsibility may be rendered very awkward.
If chance should throw a blushing, humble, tremulous female, or *implumis
bipes*, in their way, they may cross her path, and stare at, and deride her
into convulsions, as there is a *charming brutality* admissible in what is termed
polished life, which would deserve chastisement in any other.—In their
commerce with the fair they must never use the term *old*, but as applying
to wine or friendship ; nor neglect that sweetening epithet *handsome*, if they
wish for the salvation of their own credit ; yet in no instance must they
suppose them *perfect*, as it is not yet ascertained by the Magi, whether a
woman was ever finished by the Creator or not.——With these premises we
close the dogmatic placard for young gentlemen.

Twelve

'Tis the rage but to walk on the Steyne in the eve,

When the dews fall as rapid as sand through a sieve ;

Till

TWELVE GOLDEN RULES *for young Ladies of Distinction in the Year* 1796.

First—We recommend to them, to avoid all actions that are vulgar ; that is, such as prevail among the mob, and to conduct themselves, in a general sense. in such a manner as to deserve the title of being vastly singular ; a* whoever is *not* singular in this refined age, will be inevitably classed as vulgar.

Secondly—We recommend to them, in order to effect this desirable purpose, to walk like a grenadier at a review, and to strut with their arms a-kimbo, as by those means they will be enabled to make their abdominal projections the more noticeable. It should be observed, that this attitude is the *sine qua non* of a female of distinction, as the vulgar dare not assume this becoming privilege without a forfeiture of their reputation for virtue.

Thirdly—We recommend to them, whether near-sighted or not, to make an unlimited use of optical glasses, but particularly at church, during divine service, where, by an adroit and skilful management of these modish instruments, they may be lucky enough to stare the churchwarden and his family out of countenance, and happily draw an oblique reproof from the parson, which cannot fail in its operations to make them exceedingly notorious. Our male insects of distinction have in some degree forestalled this practice, but their bungling manner of abashing modesty will be quickly superseded by the ladies.

Fourthly—We recommend to them, to whisper and giggle when any person of either sex comes into a company with a trembling and humble demeanour, as this measure will increase the confusion of the visitors, and show their own superiority and firmness of nerve : to appear confused in any situation argues vulgarity in the extreme.

Fifthly—We recommend to them, to manifest a strong predilection in favor of coxcombs and fools of every description, and to sneer at men of sense and science. Some persons, whose discernment is imperfect, may be inclined to question the wisdom and expediency of this rule ; but we trust that all opposition to this injunction will be done away, when it is recollected how great a saving of time and money it will cause, by rendering the ordeal of the classics, and the ceremonies of an university, utterly nugatory and despicable.

Sixthly—We recommend to them, to be as loose in their drapery as possible, and to adhere to the present very laudable custom of fixing the cestus within three inches of their shoulders, until they are driven out of it by an

Till their clothes hang dependent, absorbing a damp,
More fatal than steams from an African swamp :

When

Act of Parliament, enforced by violence. And our reason for this urgent
desire is, that it gives an air of graceful playfulness to our fair countrywomen, and removes those barriers of restraint which formerly kept our dash-
ing young bucks at bay ; the old-fashioned and absurd habits of wearing
stays operating as a sort of armour, which checked and alarmed them on
their approaching to the duties of a salute ; whereas the present negligent
manner inspires them with an additional glow of confidence to clasp their
beauteous persons, and fills them with ideal ecstacies. And surely none but
the churlish or the prudish would hesitate to render others happy, and especially when it can be effected on such easy and advantageous terms to both
parties.

Seventhly—We recommend to them, to make as much noise and as great a
flutter as will be borne, upon their entering the boxes in a theatre : this is
perfectly fashionable, and will assuredly make them stared at by the vulgar
order of the audience, who *dare not* imitate them in their low sphere, as *they*
would be stigmatized for such freedom as impertinent, or something more
harsh and chilling : and if they should be seated in the green boxes, and
cannot attract notice by laughing, talking in a high key, or abrupt gesticula-
tions with the fan, we recommend to them to drop their cloak or shawl, as
by accident, into the pit, where JOHN BULL, who is an honest, credulous,
stupid beast, will eagerly labor to restore it to its owner *above* him, while
the ladies all around will envy such an impressive instance of notoriety.
If the cloak should be caught in its declension by a chandelier, and publicly
burned, it will prove uncommonly interesting and charming, and will pro-
bably be mentioned in all the newspapers and some magazines; verses will
be made upon the unfortunate belle, and the lady, by such means, get into
prodigious notice.

Eighthly—We recommend to those ladies, who may unhappily possess
that delicate tone of nerve which constitutes eventually the *mauvaise honte*,
to wear veils upon all ordinary occasions, as there is nothing in the wide
and long catalogue of human distresses so vulgar as even the appearance of
shame. We recommend to them to imitate the French ladies of the late
Court at Versailles, by alluring all the fashionable indolent men to join
them in parties of cards, and to preconcert the measures so neatly, as to
ease their stupid companions of a few bank notes : such steps as these are
considered as the more warrantable by the discreet, inasmuch as there is no
awkward responsibility attached to the sex, for such venial sportiveness :
besides, it is surely doing what ought to be, in transferring cash from folly

to

When the blast's south or east the spray rides in the gale,

Till you're crusted with salt like Dutch herrings for sale ;

And

to beauty—as the more you bleed a fool of his money, the fewer opportunities he will have of exposing himself, which is undoubtedly preserving a remnant of his character, obliging his family, and supporting the dignity of human nature.

Ninthly—We recommend to them, to be the first in getting into a carriage, if there be men in company, that they may have a complete occasion of showing a well-turned ancle; or if they should be proportioned like the Medicean Venus, they should affect a hoyden air, and in jumping into the phaeton or curricle, contrive to stumble upon their knee, as by that method it is an hundred to one, but the whole of one, or both limbs, is exposed to the searching eyes of the accompanying beaus, who will not fail to communicate, to all they know, as a great secret, that Miss such-a one has a d——d handsome leg. This is a sure trap to win a lover, if not a husband ; but as husbands are so seldom lovers, that is not much to be regretted. We have insinuated nothing as to those ladies who may have thick or crooked legs, as they uniformly ascend the last, upon all events, and are never seen abroad in a windy day.

Tenthly—We recommend to them, to seize every decent pretence to expose the charms of the neck and bosom ; this is satisfying the curiosity of admiration ; and to render those comfortable who are around us, is one of the first principles of good breeding. They must affect to speak in a low, monotonous, nasal tone, and as wholly independent of passion or principle ; they must write illegibly, and be sure to spell ill ; they must not be seen at any public place three times without fainting ; they must wash their mouths after dinner, and spit the cleansings in the glass, unless there should be a Turkey carpet ; they must, in that case, disgorge upon that, to show their elegant contempt of economy.

Eleventhly—We recommend to them, to assume some attractive infirmity, notwithstanding the providence and beneficence of nature may have given them a perfect organization ; and they must not, on any account whatever, admit they are in good health, as that is vulgar and abominable. The advantages resulting from an affectation of ill health and infirmity are incalculable ; it opens a timely door for a retreat from company they may either envy or hate ; and to lisp, limp, and seem half blind, have the glory of novelty with the million, who will regard them with astonishment ; but they must not remain long among them, lest their ideas should concentre in pity, and to be pitied is the next stage to being despised ! When a saturnine uncle, or a maiden aunt, chides them for irregularity, they may

reply

And when north or east, the impertinent wind
Incessantly cuts, like a razor behind :
If the nerves are too fine, the pedestrian decays ;
If not, he's lumbago'd the rest of his days.
The cold humid sod will provoke a disease,
And Catarrhs ride in ambush in every breeze.
Can a station be fitter to make Death elate,
Or suppress an incumbent who clogs an estate ;

reply good-humouredly with the end of a modern song, unless the first has land and beeves, and the latter money in the funds; in that case, they should make a low curtesy, and sneeringly promise the old folks to be gothic in future.

Twelfthly—We finally recommend to them, to support and add to the privileges of the sex upon all occasions, and, if possible, to expunge the words *honor* and *obey* from the matrimonial ceremonies. If they have any species of conveyance, they must incessantly prate of *our carriage*; and if this point is discreetly managed, there may be as much credit got with a *tilt cart* as a *sociable*. They must encourage the addresses of every male creature who has any pretension to *ton* ; and, if it is in the gift of Chance to produce a duel between any of the suitors, they will be envied by all their sex ; it will prove a matter wholly unimportant, whether the blockhead who falls is the *offender* or the *offendee* ; as it is the *eclat* of the thing, and not its propriety, that will be seriously considered !—When they bathe, they must tie the flannel shift so close to their necks, that the sea-water may not be too intrusive upon their fair bodies, as that might brace them into much rigidity of fibre : when they descend from the machines with the guide, they must wet their lower extremities by degrees, so that, if there be any humour floating in the system, it may be driven up to the head ; and it is assuredly better to have a foe infest the capital only, than every province of the state.——With these premises we close the dogmatic placard for young ladies.

ANTHONY PASQUIN.

Given at our Court of Observation, this
9th day of August 1796.

☞ We command that the above documents be read in all well-
regulated watering-places and seminaries in Great Britain,
Ireland. and the Town of Berwick upon Tweed.

Take

Take a shrew from a cuckold whom Hymen has given,

Or remove a fond spouse from his deary to heaven?

Sure all nature is twisting, our morals decay,

And every Season is dancing the hay.

Would you dream, gentle Coz, of so base a vagary?—

Both N——lk and W——m have puk'd on my dairy.

The twelve *statutes* of CHARLES each domestic derides,

And M—RR—CE's bawdry's been nail'd to my sides:

There it sticks, like a blister, to glad gaping crews,

And I sweat and I writhe while the sensual peruse.—

Some grimalkin, at midnight, pursuing his rib,

Has polluted my cap, and bedribbled my bib:

The owl's deadly screech has awak'd me with fears,

And the vagabond swallows have dung'd in my ears:

Care has furrow'd my visage with terrible ruts;

Some rats have run up me, and injur'd my guts:

How I roar'd for a trap when my proboscis smelt 'em!

How I shiver'd, and rav'd, and blasphem'd when I felt 'em!

When first I complain'd to the medical train,

Some averr'd 'twas a *scirrhus*, and others a *strain*:

Others snatching their fees, said, " You're ill, and must

    die!"

One pronounc'd I was *gravell'd*—and that was *no* lie!

Some thought, with deep woe, th' *hypogastrium* was spread!

They examin'd my *vulva*, and each shook his head!

Some swore 'twas a *scrophula* lurking unseen,

Others *scurvy*, or *lues*, or something between:

" Take the *Syrup de Velnos*," all urg'd, " and be clean:"

And

And before on what ail'd me these dolts could decide,
The vermin had eaten one third of my side !—
I was courted, last Lammas, by MARLBOROUGH HOUSE,
Though he's not got a shirt, and is not worth a souse ;
He presum'd on his rank, and his being my neighbour,
His blood of the SPENCERS, and powers of labor :
But my virgin affections he never could steal,
For his carcase is red, and his yard's ungenteel :
No spinster would let such a monster assail her ;
By the lord, I'd as soon be in bed with a taylor !

How hard 'tis to tell what young damsels should do,
When a rakehelly bachelor banters to woo :
Should they hapless consent, then the lady's too fond ;
Should they not, then they're proud to see lovers de-
    spond.
We have passions, yet dare not conjecture they live ;
We are lib'ral, yet custom denies us to give ;
And while all other animals sate their desires,
Poor Woman's heart melts by her own pent-up fires !
And I've heard some avow, whom his H———ss thought
    clever,
That good men marry early—sagacious ones never !

My fair body is cover'd, ah me, what a shame !
With barb'rous designs, like Caractacus' frame :
The foul loves of the Gods, and their bestial enjoyments ;
Young, pert, breechless Cupids at naughty employments ;
Venus looking behind in a filthy condition ;
An old rogue with a snake, whom they call a physician ;

A swan

A swan and a hussey enfolding and billing ;

A girl ravish'd in air, but appearing half-willing ;

Nymphs, naked as Folly in Westminster-hall ;

And some near undone, yet not seeming to bawl :

At gross feats, such as these, even *Grizzle* would flout ;

Nay, the stones in my joints ope their jaws, and cry out *.

Here a patriarch might gaze, and forget how to pray ;

Here a vestal might look all her virtue away :

Here *Saint Bruno* himself would of Bathsheba dream ;

And our Queen's maids of honor ideally teem ;

Th' electrical plaster will flash on each sense,

Changing faith to loose thoughts, and those thoughts to
        offence.

This was done while I slept, by a loon clep'd REBECCA ;

Pr'ythee seize him, ye Winds ; bear the varlet to Mecca :

It is surely enough to be plagu'd with desires,

Without such a bellows to heat the soul's fires.

    Loose caricaturas are stuck on my ribs,

In the spirit all libels—the letter, all fibs :

There's PITT, as a fungus, the Crown had emitted !

There's suffering *Ierne* by BERESFORD spitted !

Farmer GEORGE and his *housewife* both cramming their pigs !

MUN BURKE making BENTINCK destroy the old whigs !

* This friendly and salutary communication between the houses is not
a circumstance of such novelty as weak persons may imagine ; nor is this
idea of the Pavilion's original, as BISHOP WATSON and JOHN WILKES
know it is thus expressed in holy writ : " *The stones shall cry out of the wall, and
the beam out of the timber shall answer it.*"—Hab. ii. 11.

E   That

That vile monster, *the Public,* o'erladen with taxes!

The rich binding Justice, and stealing her axes!

TOOKE marking the busts of our monarchs as ninnies!

Bank DIRECTORS exploring their chests for *five guineas!*

Little WILBERFORCE tickling the hope of a negro!

Fraud dancing through life like another Allegro!

The *Promont'ry of Noses,* where, clad as a mumper,

PEPPER ARDEN is seen begging hard for a thumper!

Oh bear me, meek Angels, where slander may cease;

Let my body be tranquil, my spirit have peace:

I would lodge in that row near the town's magazine *,

Were there not, at all hours, such nudities seen,

Fellows running about like Di's nymphs without smocks:

Where the devil's the constable?—where are the stocks?

Bite their toes, famish'd crabs, as they lave in the deep;

Scorch their buttocks, high Sol, till they fry and they weep:

Pr'ythee take me to Abraham's bosom to rest;

That is, if the mob have not crowded his breast.

   Lord, cousin, I'm frighten'd much worse than before;

His H———, enrag'd at our ingrates here, swore

---

* This is evidently an allusion to a certain row of houses at the west end of Brighton, called *Artillery Place,* and which have been eagerly sought after by that persecuted description of the fair sex, called *old maids.* The real motive for this predilection is a principle of piety and meditation, which they can indulge, without interruption, in a spot so sequestered; and not a meretricious disposition, as the scandalous would infer, to view the naked fellows who bathe and sport beneath their windows every morning, to the annoyance of curious matrons and peery virginity.

That

That he'd make me a *Barrack* * ;—oh heaven and earth,

Why was I created ?—why had I a birth ?

And shall my perfum'd body be made such a den ?

Pray what lady could please a whole reg'ment of men ?

Must I live like a strumpet—my name be revil'd ?

Great God ! should I prove in the issue with child,

Who would foster the babe? neither HOLLAND nor WYATT;

Yet how shall I keep such strong roisterers quiet ?

S'blood, what will become of my soul in futurity ?

I will muzzle their guns : I will bind them in surety:

Th' ORANGE family must have some small-clothes will suit
     me ;

Perhaps if I scratch 'em, the ruffians will shoot me :

I'll ne'er sleep but in trowsers ; you've some of big SAM's † ,

Would cover me close from my hips to my hams.

I have heard that the prudes of Castile have a way,

To lock up their honor by night and by day :

But suppose they should force me in sleep by surprise,

By the fist of the Virgin I'll tear out their eyes :

I will shriek till the dead rise and ask why I did it ;

I will lift up a quarry, and crush those who bid it :

I will tear ope the mountain's rough bowels, and hide me ;

I will skulk to the tomb where no sin can misguide me :

---

* This instance of the aggrieved gentlewoman's alarm was well founded,
as it was commonly believed at Brighton, at the period when this letter was
written, that the P—— had expressed himself to that effect, in consequence
of a figurative procession having occurred, which implied an unmerited insult to a lady, whom it was his duty, as a gentleman, to respect.

† A gigantic porter, formerly in the service of the P ——.

I will

I will spread desolation and horror around me ;

I will—yet pray why should my anger confound me ?

For if such is Fate's order, I think I must share it,

And I hope that my strength will be able to bear it.

Yours, till death do us part,

Brighton,
August 10*th,* 1796.   PAVILION.

ODE TO BACCHUS*.

(SUPPOSED TO HAVE BEEN WRITTEN BY MAJOR H--G-R.)

The Music select.d from Lord Kellie, Lord Mornington, Carolan, &c.

STROPHE.

ILLUSTRIOUS son of Jove and Semele,

Who once lay snug on high,

Within the muscles of your father's thigh ;

To thee we dedicate this pile,

Built for the royal tenant of your isle,

---

* On the 1st of April 1787, I dreamed and imagined the following irregular Ode, Hymn, or Orgie, was performed with all due solemnity at the Marine Pavilion, on the Steyne, at Brighthelmstone. The company present were select, and remarkable for their attachment to the purple god, to whom the saloon was consecrated. Each British Bacchanal brandished a thyrsus, spirally ornamented with festoons made of Iberian grapes and laurel, and fastened with the garters of the nymph he loved best. Mr. R-GBY officiated at this revel rout as the representative of the jolly god, bestriding a hogshead of claret : his car was drawn by Messrs. H--G-R and W--T--E, who were habited on this occasion as two young tygers When they arrived at the temporary altar, the facetious proxy for Bacchus ascended into a niche, cut in the wall for that particular purpose. Mr. R-GBY's brows were curiously decorated with a wreath of vine-leaves, gathered in the plains of Languedoc, and artfully intermingled with roses.

Who

Who must one day,

When Death shall call his powers into play,

Embrace his subjects as a monstrous family :

   Oh ! guard this consecrated haunt

      From prostitution vile, and bailiff dire ;

   The means to celebrate thy glory grant ;

   Oh ! give us fuel to support the fire *.

* It hath been believed, that the most certain and infallible way to win the esteem and affection of men is, to delight in promoting their felicity, and to obviate their necessities, provided it be done with that generous grace which is the qualifying inmate of all noble minds : yet, in despite of an opinion so amiable in its tendencies, we have to produce an instance, which proves how very unknowing that individual is, who expects a return for the most essential favors, whenever the period of ordeal may arrive, that a sense of gratitude should be manifested by deeds, and not professions. We are compelled to make these remarks, from an observation of the scandalous conduct of that political party, whom we are accustomed to call the OPPOSITION, towards their royal benefactor, and, we may almost add, victim. It is notorious to all mankind, that they were the original cause of the pecuniary embarrassments of the PRINCE of WALES: their example, their suggestions, their prodigalities, progressively seduced him from the moral standard, before he had any knowledge of human artifice ; and, in the moment of that seduction, they meanly and ruinously fattened upon his exceeding bounty : yet no sooner were those means of improvident support withheld, than they blotted all recollection of his munificence from their memories, and had the audacity to affect a pity for his diminished splendor, and publicly blamed him for having suffered himself to be their dupe and sacrifice ; they rudely cast him upon an indiscriminating society, encumbered, in a great degree, with a weighty responsibility for *their* irregularities ; they clouded his perception, but could not suppress the arguments of his heart.—It must not be admitted, that this despicable behaviour is the usual result of an infirmity in the system of man ; nor should the event be passed by, unaccompanied by such an open and general reprobation, as may mark their ingratitude, and deter others from the perpetration of such enormities. The present situation of his ROYAL HIGHNESS is wonderfully singular : both the *administration* and *opposition* seem equally to operate to his disadvantage—as, from an accurate survey of the constituent parts and principles of each, he has resolved—NOT TO JOIN EITHER.

Thus

Thus prim'd and loaded, boldly we'll advance,
And follow Pleasure in the mazy dance ;
  With jocund step we'll nimbly trip,
    As the high-mettled tribe,
    The grape's celestial joys imbibe,
  And press the goblet to the parched lip.
But, zounds! can we be sorry, sad, or sick,
Who own the influence of laughing DICK ?
Oh, RICHARD! name propitious to our cause,
To Virtue dear, and honor'd by our laws—
    Damme, now I think on't, I'll give you a toast—
        But, let me see,
        By heav'ns! I think we've three,
    Who're in themselves a host!
DICK FITZPATRICK, DICK SHERIDAN, and DICK RIGBY,
With many other DICKS that fain would big be :
    Come, charge your gaping glasses,
    High as if drinking the Parnassian lasses ;
        Come, my roaring boys, prepare,
        No *heel-taps*, no *sky-lights*—all fair :
" Oh! give us young AUGUSTUS for a friend,
" Priests without fraud, and RICHARDS without end."
But is n't it odd, my lads, we ne'er could find
The zig-zag alleys of a lady's mind ?

———

A SOLEMN ORAISON.

SOME have presum'd to roam the Cretan maze,
  When Reason only gave their Wit a clew ;
Or sweep the oozy bed of Persia's seas,
  And Hope ne'er bade the laborers adieu.

But

But none, except by Desperation fir'd,
    Have e'er relied on their restricted skill,
To gain those heights Ambition oft desir'd,
    And trace the windings of the female will,

In that frail origin of nameless deeds,
    That seat of Gladness, and that womb of Woe,
The mental olive's choak'd by noisome weeds,
    And Worth and Vanity in union grow.

There wish meets wish, and sighs succeed to sighs,
    Till each the other mutually annoys ;
There kindred Passions wrestle as they rise,
    And what the judgment claims, the heart destroys.

All-pitying Fate, who gave our race to Care,
    And touch'd with pestilence the human breath ;
Correct their system, make them wise as fair,
    And let our heaven antecede our death.

ANTISTROPHE.

Come, stretch your silver throats, my lads of wax,
    To join the *thyasus*, and glad the god ;
Let each distend his windpipe till it cracks,
    And make the heavenly brandy-merchant nod ;
That true-born Britons may be free from thinking,
And we eternally be drunk, or drinking ;
Empty the Thames, the Severn, Humber, Dee,
And bid their vile, insipid waters flee ;
Then exercise a privilege divine,
And fill the boundless vacuum with wine.

Guard

Guard us, blithe deity, whene'er we sleep,

Oh, lead us from the dangers of the deep *.

If ever I forget thy recent kindness,

May black Perdition strike me dark with blindness,

May heaven suppress the greenness of my youth,

May I be ravish'd by the naked Truth †.

STROPHE.

May spinsters, impell'd by Love's flame, flock around us,

May the demons of Apathy never confound us;

    May we live all our lives,

      With profusion of treasure,

    And kiss widow'd wives,

      Till we fill up Love's measure :

Be this carousal lauded by that strumpet,

Wondrous Renown, till she has burst her trumpet.

  We'll scale the empyrean, cleave the yielding air,

Embrace old Jove's proud paralytic bride,

  Or, in a fit of high-wrought fury, tear

The blue-ey'd Hebe from the Thunderer's side.

  We'll ballot DEATH among us, he's so clever,

He loves *the turf*, my boys, and prompts our ends ;

When *one of us*, he may not smite his friends,

  And we may live—for ever ! ! !

---

* Here the MAJOR is supposed to allude to his providential escape in the summer of 1787, from the fangs of a shark, on the coast of Brighthelmstone, which seized him by the *glutæi* while he was bathing with the P——. When the MAJOR had recovered from his consternation, and solemnly thanked the gods for the preservation of his ——, he swore, upon the holy evangelists, that the voracious fish had a human countenance, and was as like JACK MANNERS as one pea is to another.

† This is highly picturesque of the MAJOR's well-founded apprehensions, when presiding at the ADAM and EVE CLUB in Marylebone.

Then,

Then, then, we'll roar, and give the bully welcome,
The grave shall think it is not he, but hell come :—
Then we'll sweep Tartarus, make evil worse,
Ravish the ghosts, and empty Croesus' purse ;
Burn Minos' wig, roll Charon in the kennel,
And send grim Cerberus to hunt with MEYNEL :
We'll break the cynic's lantern all to shivers,
Make *Lusitania*'s hogsheads run like rivers ;
Tear out the leaves from Retribution's ledger,
Seize callow Schism by the skirts, and fledge her :
We'll make the elements all bend to suit us,
Embrazen Hope, and let no soph confute us :
Twist the vast linch-pin of th' erratic planet,
Illume Love's fane, and bid the Muses fan it :
We'll teaze the Cardinal Sisters till they fret,
And catch sweet spinsters in a silken net ;
Emboss our flagons with the smockless graces,
And crush those loons who blush to show their faces :
We'll brain the Magi, terrify the watch,
And make the Privy Council sing a catch ;
Ope Fortune's door, and bid the million enter,
And chain th' illiberal to creation's centre.

When high AUGUSTUS mingles with the dust,
As all of us, my toping gallants, must ;
TAYLOR * shall have the hens, and chicks, and geese ;
D—BY a cock, and WATTY WYNNE the cheese :

W—DH—M

* Mr. M. A. TAYLOR, from his prodigious knowledge of the law, and
constant practice in the courts, looks, at least, to be Lord Chancellor, if his
party get into their hands the helm of state ; but when that event may
take place, it is as difficult to ascertain, as the point at which the last dying

F   sound

W—DH—M shall hunt the bucks for WELTJIE's spit :
We'll send the milk, when skimm'd, to BILLY PITT :
BROOKS shall have half *the pigeons* ; ROSE *the muck ;*
C—TH—E *a cart* ; and each M. D. *a duck !*
We'll give *the hogs* to L—GGE, R—D *the bull ;*
Turnips to YOUNG, Sir JOHN S—CL—R *the wool :*
We'll send th' Imperial Gen'ral FUNK *the waggons ;*
The Ship and Castle taps shall have *the flagons :*
We'll give *the cream* to SHERRY for his jokes ;
The LORDS OF SESSION shall have *all the yokes.*
We'll give *the scythe* to Time, *the rope* to REEVES !
AD—R *the goats*—to MELLISH all *the beeves !*
Fortune shall take *the ass,* AN——CH *the rams !*
THE POOR THE GRAIN, and ROWLAND HILL *the lambs !*
CANNING shall have *the whey*—Mark-lane *the scales,*
Phœbus the steeds, and Eton School *the flails :*
BURKE and JOHN KETCH may share *the whips* by halves!
And *Cam* and *Isis* shall have *all the calves !*
Each rood shall slumber fallow for a year,
Unsuck'd by wheat, or oats, or beans, or bere :
And then we'll pay, my boys, each cumbrous debt,
And tell the gaping world, A FARM'S TO LET !

    What say you, lads, shall we exert our powers,
Arrest old Time, and subjugate his hours ?

sound may expire. It is much to be apprehended that, though he came
a *chicken* into opposition, he will wear *cock's spurs* for many years before he
is *master of his walk.* Being rather *light,* he is never *pitted* in a *grand battle,*
though generally produced in the *byes* ; but being *under weight,* even there
he cannot be depended upon. At present he is used as a *sparring cock,* just
to try the temper of those of the *grand main,* on whom the success of the
day depends.

                                  Shall

Shall it be said that we despair ?
  Not I ; nor you ; nor you !
We'll seize that bold usurper, Care,
  And beat him black and blue ;
    And, d'ye hear, *I'll bet the gods,*
        Ten to one,
    Or give them—*the long odds*—
        The thing is done.

  Thou jocund child of Semele,
  Protect our jovial family—
  What means this genial light,
  Chasing the inmates of the sombrous night ?
        See, see, the god descends !
        BACCHUS and we are friends ;
By heavens ! he's taking off his jacket,
I'll be his *bottle-holder,* while you support the racket.
  Damme, LADE, the god for a hundred ;
        Where's the *spanish ?*—Done ! Done !
        Here's your fun :
    Though his stomach's stor'd,
    And he has got his beer on board,
  The boy, when groggy, never blunder'd.
  Now begin the chorus,
  To give him *spunk* to drive the dog before us !

GRAND CHORAL BURST.

Come, *spiflicate* that scoundrel CARE,
Gruel him, bruise him, never fear ;
Oh ! may the powers gymnastic
Make the ruddy youth elastic :

Blood! never fear him, though he swaggers,

See already how the villain staggers!

Don't *give it in—peg away,*

His H——ss will see fair play :

That's your sort—wipe his jowl,

He's bottom ;—he's a soul.

With a *handful* of *bones* let his mazzard be cramm'd ;

He a *Pugilist !*—he be d——d !

Stand up to him stoutly, and *tip him a straight one,*

Now *rattle his head,* for the slave has a great one ;

Cross buttock the vagabond, *trip up* his *creepers,*

Darken his daylights, and *pepper his peepers ;*

Now at his *bread-basket,* just in the nick there ;

See, the dog turns his breech about, give him a kick there.

Zounds! here's a fight should be sung by Apollo,

For BACCHUS will beat the old reprobate *hollow.*

> Now try your might,
>
> *Touch him under the left ribs*—that's right,
>
> He's broke his jaw,
>
> Huzza!
>
> Repeat your blows,
>
> There he goes ;
>
> *Sew up his eyes,*
>
> There he lies, and dies,

Never, never, never, never, never more to rise * !

---

* As this poetical Olio is confessedly the issue of a dream, and as it *is not possible* that the lady could have acquired all these pugilistic phrases intuitively, it must be supposed, that she had previously heard them bandied about in conversation, beneath her roof, by some of the *heads* of the *opposition,* who were *amateurs* of the noble science of boxing.

ANOTHER SERIOUS EPISTLE

FROM

CARLTON HOUSE

TO

THE PAVILION AT BRIGHTON.

DEAR PAV.

Your *ironical* Ode, the loose fancy combin'd,
As a novel, amuses the overstrain'd mind :
Though varlets, like tendrils, impressively free,
Clung around his fair trunk, they've not injur'd the tree;
Then let not HYPOCRISY sneer so malign,
Or draw forth her snakes—the *auspicium*'s benign :
No envy, no meanness could cleave to his will,
And his soul ever scorn'd adaptation to ill.
When the throne's his estate, and he issues his thought,
He'll irradiate the realm, and be all that he ought.
The imperial eagle shall proudly ride o'er him ;
All humanity hail, and all Britons adore him.

The caprices of Fashion are wondrous indeed,
And the wrigglings of Folly oft make my heart bleed :
Though not old as the hills, I remember the day,
When St. James's Park was the scene to display

All

All the beauty of Britain ; then beaus with long sleeves,
And long skirts, and long stories, made love to their Eves ;
Made their vows to their Daphnes, who each kept her man
At the end of her hoop, and the end of her fan :
Beyond that, not a Tarquin could venture ;—but now
The fond sluts let 'em buss, in that moment they bow :
No dread of destruction enfeebles their act ;—
Nay, they'd kiss without blushing, and publish the fact :
Were they plac'd where the dragon withheld lawless fruit,
They would each munch a pippin, and poison the brute :
The Tabby's fell obloquy's now lost its force,
Each seems bad, till you know her companion, who's worse :
Has thought fled the vile inconsiderate elves ?
Pray who'll honor that sex that don't honor themselves ?

 The metropolis now an excrescence is grown ;
It is spread like the evil—'tis gone *out of town !*
But the realm, as a body, no health can impart,
The north road's the *aorta,* and that is the heart ;
Whence it forces vile blood all th' anatomy over,
From Snowdon to Caithness, from Penzance to Dover :
It lies stretch'd on the main, and fortuitous driven,
Like a wallowing monster insulting high heaven :
It creates its own vermin, who crawl o'er its face,
Bellowing loud of their rights while they worship disgrace !
It's diseas'd and decrepit, old, wicked, and sly,
And as pregnant with humours as dogs in July.
When an ulcer is burst on its navel or jaw,
Its *pediculi* suck it, and call it *a Spa* ;

Raise

Raise irregular huts to confederate thick,
Make their faith their perdition, and drink themselves *sick !*
  You've a Dutchess, I'm told, dress'd as Puritans would ;
And some dairy-maids clad as our dutchesses should :
Though in either 'tis madness to rush to be blam'd,
Yet they're *privately pleas'd* that they're *publicly sham'd.*
'Tis the rage to be noted, makes Folly inclin'd
To laugh loud at the altar, and ride o'er the blind :
Many catch, e'en in guilt, at the general gaze,
And seem blest in proportion as each can amaze :
But whene'er Observation shall cease to descry,
Notoriety'll pine, and our foplings will die.
  How many are curs'd in the strife to be gay !
How many but live at the death of the day !
How the heart's soft emotions are slain by excess !
For that nymph has no slave who would commonly bless !
Though she blazons thus roseate, and prattles so fine,
Her *health* is all—*rouge,* and her *spirits—bad wine.*
We're egregiously taking our joys upon trust,
Till the farce is compress'd, and we moulder in dust :
In living beyond what's prescrib'd for our pow'rs,
We absorb true delight to anticipate hours.—
Yet who gains by thus marring the night and the morn ?—
'Tis abridging the use of a day that's unborn !
Though they knit in the dance, and are dreadfully glad,
'Twill predim their bright eyes, and make Beauty's soul sad,
How brittle's existence !—how futile our health !
How deceptive is grandeur !—how flippery our wealth !

Some

Some are cut down by Time, while half shav'd and half
　　lather'd;—

But old Q *. fully mown, to his fathers is gather'd.

Ah! he died like a saint, though he'd smack'd of the sinner:

He's snatch'd from Life's feast, having mumbled his dinner.

Thus

* *A* Monody *recited at the* Jockey Club, *on the*
　　supposed Demise of good old Q.

Non mortes, sed mores, faciunt martyres.　St. Austin.

Snug, but done up, a shepherd grey
　　Must rot beneath the sod;
Cherubs, in cotton wrap his heart,
　　And bear it to *bis* God.

The gem of Piccadilly's lost,
　　The first or last of men.
Take him, bright heav'n! *Newmarket* roar'd;
　　And *Epsom* groan'd, Amen!

Spadille and *Basto* hung their ears;
　　Pam snivell'd and look'd sad;
The *Queen of Hearts* with horror gaz'd,
　　And all the *Knaves* were mad.

He's borrow'd—he's gone home—he's dish'd!
　　He's thrown—his race is done!
He's had—he's smash'd—he's tipt all nine!
　　He's spilt—he's cut and run!

He's will'd Dame Phillips all his *skin*;
　　To Liptrap all his spirit;
His brains St. Luke's—his blood to Brookes—
　　To B—thby all his merit.

When ragged Virtue, 'neath a hedge,
　　His dexter eye survey'd
Begash'd and gor'd by sportive Fate,
　　He cheer'd the half-clad maid:

The beatitudes were all his own;
　　He copied Israel's Kings;
Cover'd her nakedness with care,
　　And fed her with good things.

More

Thus, you see, Magnanimity's ta'en a peg lower :

Think of this, you pert minx—seek Repentance, and know
    her.

All the nap may be worn from the superfine drapery ;

The young Day may be chas'd by a Night black and vapoury:

Maudlin Juno might perish for ripping Jove's breeches !

Agile Hermes be hung, who'd ta'en Plutus's riches !

Ceres' barn be unroof'd—Ocean swallow our cities !

Old Mars lose his halberd, and Phœbus his ditties !

Th' exciseman seize Bacchus with tubs of *run* gin !

Lean Hope punt at *Pharo,* and yet never win !

D'ye expect, you vile jade, like the Sybarite crew,

To sleep but on vi'lets, and drink roses' dew ?

Your betters can suffer, and not yield a tear ;

Zounds ! I've been *in a pillory* many a year !

Thank your stars for a your cates—ring not Misery's bell,

There are few bricklayers' daughters can live half so well.

Yours, &c.

Pall Mall,
August 13*th,* 1796.

CARLTON HOUSE.

More like Samaritan than Thane,
    Eschewing mortal sin,
He grop'd to find the lady's wound—
    And pour'd his balsam in.

Ah ! lifeless, luckless, starless Q.!
    Cupid's *bonne bouche* and dread ;
The nymphs, clep'd Cyprian, shall trim,
    And make him *decent*—dead !

That is, if Death, or Hell, or Jove,
    Or tipstaff—which you will—
While ladies finger his remains,
    Can make the Peer—lie still.

G

A DIDACTIC EPISTLE

FROM

SAINT JAMES'S PALACE

TO

THE PAVILION AT BRIGHTON, GREETING.

MY DEAR PAV.

CARLTON HOUSE show'd me your complaints;
You muſt not think that men are saints:
Besides, you minx, you're much too young
To judge of life, and right and wrong:
Not but your morals please me much,
Though, to be frank, they are not such
As fits the age—pray learn from me,
Who've seen more years than you or she;
And though *extrema senectute,*
I've some remains of manly beauty:
So many throng'd here from the north,
They broke my back last JUNE the *fourth.*
When prelates die, I'm so berook'd,
D. D.'s have gorg'd me till I puk'd;
And when reg'mental chiefs expire,
With scarlet mobs I'm all on fire.
I once, like PEPYS, jalap'd all,
The gross, the slender, short, and tall:
Mark the reverse of mortal pride;
Now kings carouse where lepers died!—

Though

Though CARLTON whimpers not, like you,

She has her cares, and those not few—

W—T—E and FITZ had ample claws,

And hunger, that ne'er knew a pause;

Though to be *useful* they were taken,

They ate, not sav'd, their master's bacon:

Ere lying Rumour's trump was blowing,

And he'd a crust just worth bestowing,

They've stuck to what could scarce a mouse hold,

The *Tom* and *Phillis* of the household:

In lovely sympathy they tarried,

How piteous they were never married!

But when the storm began to lower,

And little Villany had power,

Each, with the instinct of a rat,

Waddled away surcharg'd with fat;

Wish'd that his reason might be stronger,

And sign'd their prey would last no longer;

Became *most insolently kind*,

And mark'd his woes to sooth his mind!

Then, that his pangs might *cease with life*,

They turn'd him over to—HIS WIFE *!

But

* An AUTHENTIC SOLUTION to the ROYAL MYSTERY.

WHOEVER impelled the PRINCESS of WALES, during the zenith of a recent misunderstanding, to be systematic in the exposure of herself at the Opera, and of herself and her child at the windows at Carlton House, and the balcony looking into St. James's Park, and riding in her carriage, with the child at the window, every Sunday only, in Hyde Park, committed an irreparable offence, inasmuch as it bore the appearance of wishing indirectly to raise and stimulate a party in the nation against the PRINCE, which, we trust, was not her intention. If it were necessary to reclaim an irregular

husband

But to the statutes I'd enforce ;

I'm old, and garrulous of courfe :

Urge

husband (which we will not admit to be the case in the present instance), that demeanour is assuredly *not* the way to effect the measure.
The PRINCESS, as a *lady* and a *stranger*, deserves infinite consideration with
every delicate and gallant mind ;—yet, great as those considerations are,
even they should be subordinate to truth. The horrid report, so un-
remittingly propagated, that the PRINCE had used the Princess ill, in any
sense whatever, was false, wicked, impossible, and infamous.—The serious
epoch is not perhaps very far off, when *all* that the Princess has so unwisely
communicated to LORD and LADY CHOLMONDELY will be divulged ;
and it will be then, and not till then, that the mystery will be duly understood, and the reputation of the PRINCE blanched even from the suspicion
of meaning improperly.—That great Personage, whose advice the lady has
thought it expedient to receive and obey, has managed his own domestic
concerns too incorrectly, if not unhappily, to form the required example in
such a dilemma ; and, putting his heart out of the dispute, we are inclined
to believe his judgment is not of the very highest order. The morality of
their MAJESTIES and the DUTCHESS of YORK having never been questioned, it remains to inquire how, and in what manner, those illustrious
Personages have acted towards their fair relative :—we could " a tale
unfold" of the deepest importance, but, from prudential motives, shall
commit the developement to time ;—at present we can positively and
honorably assert, that the PRINCE of WALES is a—*very injured man !*

We can entertain no doubt, but, from the commencement of that negotia-
tion, which inclined the PRINCE of WALES to withdraw his support from
the *opposition*, and confer with Mr. PITT upon subjects of the deepest importance to his own immediate felicity, and the welfare of the state, there
were persons secretly employed in the fabrication of embryo measures, which
were to be progressively brought forth and enforced, as the exigencies of a
crooked policy might require ; measures fraught with a mischievous calcula-
tion, upon what human imbecility might effect under the pressure of particular evils ; while the adverse parties, most interested in the completion of the
plot, cherished a base expectation that the disappointment of passion might
lead on to the commission of a palpable error, which their subtlety might
aggravate, and render established and irrevocable.

When the PRINCE consented to marry the PRINCESS of BRUNSWICK, it
is believed there were persons who were more intimately acquainted with
the actual state of that curious lady's heart, than the gentleman who was
destined to lead her to the altar ; and if they possessed that knowledge, it
becomes a moral question, whether they should have done exactly what
they did ? As his Royal Highness was denied (but perhaps not necessarily)

the

Urge what I may to the aggriev'd,

I'm like Cassandra, ne'er believ'd ;

E'en

the opportunity of knowing the PRINCESS, in any other way than through the medium of report, it was directly incumbent upon those who presented the choice, to have been unequivocally confirmed in the idea, that the lady's qualifications were suited to his disposition, and analogous to his character ; as otherwise, what conclusion could be expected, but a wretched indifference for each other, if not the wreck of happiness for ever ?

We will suppose an hypothetical Princess, who possessed a portion of craft incompatible with her years, and hostile to moral order ; who, in conjunction with *impassioned* agents in *her own* country, and agents *without passions* in another, arranged a scheme to possess eventually the sovereignty of a foreign nation by marriage ; and in the *presumed issue* of that nuptial intercourse, considered the *admitted pledge* as a consummation of her dearest desire ; which, by dexterously managing, between the *concealed disgust* of her husband (the cause of which his honor would not permit him to divulge), and the public confidence, would lead, through indirect avenues, to a point where she might be enabled to make his gentlemanly and delicate forbearance a collateral, but sufficient argument to substantiate her own superior purity of character, in order that, when the predilection was mature, and which the attributes of her sex would enforce, she might rule, unchecked by any power even equal to her own—that she might sate her large stomach of ambition, and be QUEEN SOVEREIGN instead of QUEEN CONSORT. If there ever were such atrocious beings, we have only to pray that they might be completely unmasked ;—such personages would not be dissimilar to the *interested wanton*, who, having gulled a credulous and sympathetic companion of an ample and undeserved settlement, snaps her fingers in his face to finish the insidious procedure.

Perhaps it may not be unessential to the nation, to be informed of the following events : how far, or in what manner, they apply to existing circumstances, every reader may discover.——About the year 1756, two PRINCESSES of BRUNSWICK, aunts to the present PRINCESS of WALES, came from Germany to this country, under the idea, that one of them might be married to his present Majesty, then PRINCE of WALES ; but the ladies returned to the continent without fulfilling *that* point of their *desires*. DODINGTON, in his Diary, relates an anecdote of the PRINCESS DOWAGER of WALES, that is not altogether uninteresting at this moment ; he says, that she drew the portrait of that PRINCESS of BRUNSWICK, as follows :—" I dislike the intended alliance extremely : the young woman was said to be handsome, with good qualities, and appropriate wit, &c.; but if she takes after her mother she will never do here : the DUKE of BRUNSWICK, indeed, her father, is a very worthy man ; but her mother is the

most

E'en though each circumstance I tell
Were all as true as heat's in hell !

Yet,

most meddling, intriguing, and also the most sarcastical, satirical person in the world, and will always *make mischief* wherever she comes.—Such a character would not do with our GEORGE ; it would not only hurt him in his public, but make him uneasy in his private situation."—We must hope, nevertheless, that there is no similitude between the AUNT and the NIECE ; as, in these new-fangled times, it might in a future reign, if not during the present, be attended with very injurious effects to public order, and the cause of monarchy, in this country.

In all the conflicts of party, in all the divisions and subdivisions of social sentiment, in this country, the virtues of her Majesty have never been questioned : she possesses an undisputed empire in the hearts of Britons; her laudable enforcements of the duties of a wife and mother will render her an exemplary point to future generations ; she has nurtured the lovely Princesses agreeably to the will of heaven : and would this illustrious lady, who has so high an idea of the dignity of propriety in her sex, openly espouse the cause of the PRINCE of WALES, if she did not *know* him to have been most seriously injured, and most cruelly insulted?—Yet it is not her Majesty alone who resists this tide of obloquy ; but the King, and all the Royal Family, excepting a certain Duke and his discomfited son !—A young lady, situated like her who is the immediate subject of this national appeal, might have many foibles, although as chaste as Diana :—she might be *irregularly* ambitious—she might be haughty—she might be ignorant—she might expect, upon the demise of the King, to be even something more than QUEEN CONSORT, at least while her infant lived : that might be her latent aim !—she might endeavour to raise a NEW PARTY for that purpose, and play off *the existing parties* as best suited her desires. All this might be, may be, but should not be.

Those persons who are permitted to domesticate with his Majesty, know that HE is as much disgusted at the conduct of the PRINCESS of WALES, as the Queen, the Princesses, the DUTCHESS of YORK, and all the Royal Brothers ; and this strong disapprobation materially originated from the following circumstance :—When the PRINCESS of WALES mentioned certain terms of accommodation, the PRINCE of WALES cordially acceded to them, and that in a manner so thoroughly handsome, that the King rapturously acknowledged the Prince had behaved *like a man of honor :* but mark ! when it was believed that the embarrassments were wholly done away, the PRINCESS of WALES assumed a different feature, and dictated *more* terms, and those of such a tendency, as could not be complied with by any man of spirit. When his Majesty heard this, he was so deeply affected and hurt,

that

> Yet, if oppos'd by dunce or devil,
> Truth will, like water, find its level.

Some

that he wrote her a letter, informing her, the PRINCESS of WALES, that, as he thought her conduct improper, he would never more interfere, if she did not comply with the original terms. The only comment to be made on this extraordinary proceeding is, that she has seldom been with any of the Royal Family since, but upon *cold* visits, and SHE WAS FORBID TO PAY THEM ANY VISITS AT WEYMOUTH.

There can be nothing more evident, than that *the complicated and important plot*, which has been *managed* with such satanic address and subtlety, meant nothing less than to reduce the importance of THE WHOLE NATIVE ROYAL FAMILY. The diabolical struggles to murder the reputation of LADY JERSEY, were to be only preparatory to a more comprehensive scene of degradation of a higher nature, and a more terrible aspect; but to the introduction or completion of which, that lady's fall was peculiarly necessary: it was to form the seeming basis on which the parties were to stand for the *assassination* of even GREATER NAMES!—Lesser instruments were employed in this solemn piece of villany, and *urged* to use a zeal heretofore uncongenial with their nature. There is no truth more glaring, that that the people of this country have derived the greater portion of their miseries from that hungry credulity, which is their characteristic and their bane: and their positiveness, or rather their brutal pride, is so extraordinary, that they would sooner become sacrifices to misconception, than evince a disposition to acknowledge that they had been deceived. The *virgin impression* of a tale loudly told, however false in its premises and ruinous in its tendencies, is hardly ever eradicated from the general mind;—what was originally believed can scarcely be eventually removed. That high principle of action, or *mens conscia recti*, which is manifested in a silent disdain of little foes, and, as it might be expected, would produce the best effect, most lamentably engenders the very worst consequences;—what the aggrieved party meant to exhibit as the supreme sense of contempt for an idle malediction, is supposed by the vulgar, and insisted on by the interested, to be a tacit confession of the imputed imperfection:—thus the human character becomes immolated by the direct means which all the nobly virtuous would exercise in similar circumstances.

It cannot be supposed, that the DUKE of GLOUCESTER, who is the brother of his Majesty, and the uncle of the PRINCE of WALES, could be *impelled* to the prosecution of any indiscretion that might possibly injure the great interests of his august family;—the magnanimity and wisdom of this Prince, both in public and *private*, forbid the supposition—if he indeed resembled

sembled

Some men of failings make a jest,

In secret by themselves possess;

Hoping,

sembled the DUKE of B—— in Germany, who is said to dine daily with his mistress at the head of his table, and in the presence of his wife; but that is impossible—the DUKE of GLOUCESTER is so honored and respected by his truly amiable dutchess, that he *can* eat, drink, speak, or sleep with her whenever *he* pleases; and that he can and has done so for the last *fifteen years*, LADY ALMERIA CARPENTER can determine: it is true, that, to save trouble, she becomes occasionally the mutual messenger to both; but that is merely to keep up the nuptial farce in the establishment, and is uncommonly agreeable and amusing *to all the parties*.

It cannot be supposed, that PRINCE WILLIAM of *Gloucester* can be in any way inimical to the PRINCE of WALES, as *his* education must have been perfectly politic and moral; his *father* being notorious for *his sagacity*, and his *mother* for her *humility, candour*, and *forbearance*. It may be true, that PRINCE WILLIAM has been paying his addresses to *all* the Princesses, and it may be likewise true, that all have rejected him; yet that might not curdle the milk of his amiable disposition, as there is LORD M—TM—s in similar or more adverse circumstances, and yet his philosophy was never ruffled, nor his *habits* ever changed!

It cannot be supposed that Mr. CHARLES GREVILLE, son-in-law to the DUKE of PORTLAND, and who is under-secretary to the Sovereign, would be severely vindictive towards his royal master's family, but particularly the Heir-apparent of the realm!—as such argument and bitterness might be considered wonderfully irreconcileable in an official person thus situated; and it is not greatly remote from our usual comprehension to believe, that such a direction of manners and language would not be very palatable to the King, or very advantageous to that state, of which his noble relation is an extraneous *buttress*, and himself a *post*—we regret that we cannot apply the term *pillar* to either.

It cannot be supposed, that the MARQUIS de NOAILLES, who is a noble mendicant in this island, would so far hazard his personal convenience, as to unite in the propagation of such disastrous calumny; and especially at this momentous era, when it is not only imagined, but felt and understood, that any indistinct motion or eccentricity of an emigrant from France, not *perfectly consistent*, or, in plainer and more unequivocal matter, *not satisfactory* to Mr. PITT, would not only be extremely detrimental to the peace and fortune of such an improvident alien, but, according to probability and proof, operate as the cause to have him incontinently and forcibly driven from the protection of that legislature, whose tolerance, it would be argued, he had forfeited and abused!

It

Hoping, by aid of timely cunning,
To turn the streams of social funning.

I know

It cannot be supposed, that, of all the bipeds which amble about this populous city, Tommy Onslow would be the manikin to prattle disrespectfully of the Prince : it cannot be believed that a creature apparently so harmless, could have any perfidiousness in his soul; the size of which, if analogous to his frame, cannot have room for more than two passions, and those are presumed to be, the *love of himself*, and the *love of his ponies*. This amazing *little* gentleman was never known to be envious but once in his existence ; and the miserable object of that shabby emotion was—*a stage-coachman !*

It cannot be supposed, that Mrs. Robinson, or the *Perdita*, or the *lame Sappho*, or what you will, would, in the moment that she is receiving an annuity of five hundred pounds from the bounty of the Prince, unite in the interested cabal who labor to tarnish his good name ;—she should have remained, at least, inactive during the crooked progress of the floating falsehood. How lamentable it would be to admit, that the force of *any species of jealousy* can awaken impertinences, and connect *ideal events*, for the unwarrantable purpose of suppressing an unoffending individual whom we envy, but whom it was intended by Truth and Nature we should respect !—But it is not possible—Mrs. Robinson's morality cannot be so far unhinged.

When the Dutchess of York arrived in this country, she did not adopt the plan and manners of a certain young gentlewoman, with respect to the Duke, her husband, who was at that period neither remarkable for his constancy or temperance : he was but too much inclined to consume the night at Brookes's, in those circles, where an uxorious severity is seldom the theme of admiration.—Had the Dutchess, on those probing occasions, assumed that *fierté* and folly, and restless spirit of complaining, which constitutes the weakness of another, instead of pursuing the mild duties of an affectionate wife, that happy pair would have been now at a fashionable distance.— But what was that charming lady's conduct in an interim, when love, and delicacy, and regret, must all have had a temporary influence in her heart ?—Did she upbraid him ?—No !—Did she exhibit any symptom of resentment ?—No ; for resentment never had a residence in her placid bosom : actuated by the fervor of hope, and chastened by feminine complaisance, she was accustomed to sit in her carriage, and wait for the Duke, with the most fascinating resignation ; and by those soothing and endearing manners she soon accomplished all her wishes, which are found in the blisses of domestication, and the entire affection of

I know the Cabinet right well,

Yet half I know I dare not tell :

Oh

her loving and beloved husband !—The Dutchess of York is a model for imitation as a *Princess* —her Majesty is a model for imitation as a *Royal Consort.*

In which of the ages of the world the barbarous privilege was assumed, of compelling the youth of both sexes to intermarry, independent of the genial emotions of sympathy, we know not ; but whenever it did occur, it was a moment fatally ominous to human peace.—Just heaven ! who would be a Prince, if it was in the power of a governing or capricious statesman, from motives of ambition or *hatred*, or as the result of an inexplicable jargon, which he may denominate policy, to say to him, *Thou shalt marry that individual !* and being married, become eminently responsible for the performance of those undescribable exactions of nuptial tenderness, which have their origin in the heart, and not the judgment, and which the statutes may verbally, but cannot practically, enforce ? if it is possible that disobeying a sacrament can be in any degree venial, in situations of superlative distress, that might be a case where the sting of the violation may be absorbed in the mightiness of the cause !——If such is the fettered state of Princes,

" I would sooner be a toad, and live

Upon the vapour of a dungeon."

We are penetrated with affliction and indignation in the survey of those political mazes in which the Prince of Wales has been seduced, by the ignorance of some, and the artifices of others : a situation where it was impossible that any could walk strait or certainly ; and yet, where to be innocently indirect, would be pernicious to *his* best and primary interests. Those who have the honor of knowing his Royal Highness must declare, that his sensibility is most keenly poignant ;—then why should he be exclusively denied the very essential power to elect a lady for his wife, who, it would be expected, should reside in his heart for ever ?—The Duke of York had his choice, and it was such as is approved by God and man.— The Duke of Gloucester had his choice, and a blessed choice he made ! —but the amiable and persecuted Prince was to have none : a cold-blooded cabinet sent a lady's portrait for his idolatry ; and his eternal joy was to be dependant upon the imagination of a mercenary artist.—The momentous *douceur* that was to accelerate and accompany this deed of s—f m——r was, *the complete liquidation of his debts ;* that was the basis on which this extraordinary connexion was founded ; and that promise was never fulfilled ! When the discussion took place on this ambiguous point, his eyes were open to all

his

Oh could I change them, while they're sitting,
To so many *old women* knitting*!

They

his perils; he found himself insulated and opposed, *with equal sincerity* and good manners, by the ADMINISTRATION and the OPPOSITION: the common pretext was, a retrospective and weeping consideration for the national finances; and all who know the exquisite friendship of Mr. PITT for the PRINCE of WALES, and the iron habits of economy in Mr. FOX and *his* friends, will assuredly give them *due credit* for the asseveration.

As the PRINCESS is so pertinacious in the exhibition of herself and her infant, at the windows of her palace, and that in attitudes so expressively indicative of " moody melancholy," we think that Mr. WEST could not employ his talents to more advantage, than in pourtraying her Royal Highness as a *German Madonna:* the lady has an air of celestial meditation, not dissimilar to the Holy Mother in the *Villa Berghese.* We do not know that it would be irregular, if she went to the theatres, and had a play commanded by the ROYAL INFANT, on the same evening that their MAJESTIES visited the other house: even if the influence of custom were against the measure, who can say but the noblest purposes might be brought about by the brilliant essay!

It may be physically and morally possible, that, were we to take a peep in the ROYAL NURSERY at CARLTON HOUSE, we might behold *a rara-show,* or petticoat regiment, thus adroitly ordered: viz. the PRINCESS and the ROYAL INFANT smiling in the fore ground, while the DUTCHESS of L——DS was warming a clout!—the MARCHIONESS of S——D wiping the child's bottom with a tattered copy of the *Salique law!*—LADY S—SE—Y adjusting the cradle!—LADY C———Y expounding *the whole Duty of Man* to her august mistress!—LADY W——Y showing with tears where the baby was chafed!—LADY W—IL—CE reading that part of *Paradise Lost* where EVE is devouring the fruit of disobedience, and causing her husband's perdition in the garden of life!—MISS LA C—STR on her knees administering pap!—MRS. F—FZ——T giving the youngling *la carte blanche* on the holy Father!—MOTHER C—WI—Y learning *Gamma's* speech upon the birth of Elizabeth, in order to repeat it to the PRINCESS when she is enabled *to understand it!*—and thus they might be occupied, until MOTHER BOWRES made

---

* There is a cursed insinuation in this idea, which merits public reprobation; as, if it means any thing, it is to declare, that the same number of old women would be equally advantageous to the empire.—If the writer of this too familiar passage remains unpunished by the aggrieved parties, it can only arise from an apprehension of *pulling an old house over their heads!*

They hang together great and small,
Like stairs built geometrical ·

Thus

made the festal signal, by seizing the Royal Infant in her arms, and chaunt-
ing right merrily the following harmless *parody* on Swift's ballad; while
the noble gossips knitting hands, danced, and laughed, and sung around
her during the chorus :

The Baby shall sit on a throne,
   To be controll'd by no man ;
And then its own nursey shall be
   A—*necessary* woman :
It shall *look down* on the mob ;
   It shall sit at Britain's steerage :
It shall have sops for the law,
   And *caps* for *an infant peerage !*

GENERAL DANCE AND CHORUS.

We will go *up, up, up,*
   And THEY shall go *down, down, downy ;*
When *both* its PAPAS are dead,
   The chicken shall have a CROWNY !

It shall have a *rattle* and *bib,*
   That's a *sceptre* and *robe* I mean-a;
It shall never be *Cæsar's* rib,
   But it shall be a QUEEN-a :
Each knave and each pimp of the realm
   Shall petition to be its lackey ;
And those who think *little* of GOD
   Shall kiss its nacky, nacky

GENERAL CHORUS, &c.

It shall get TEA from the East ;
   It shall get *sweets* from the West-a ;
It shall add tythes to the church,
   And make its own D——y a jest-a :
Poor PEGGY shall bring it her blood ;
   JOHN BULL shall take care of its mammy ;
PADDY 'll send it some usquebaugh,
   And its nursey shall have a drammy !

GENERAL CHORUS, &c.

There's

Thus brother gradual raises brother
By *slight attachments* to each other.

> There's *a big party* with PITT;
>   And another with CHARLEY FOXY;
> But we'll have a *pyebald cabal*,
>   Made of remnants by COUNT T——N's *doxy!*
> Then PITT may chop logic and rave;
>   Fox, SHERRY, and he be allied-a;
> But we'll get on the cock-horse ourselves,
>   And nobody else shall ride-a!

GENERAL CHORUS, &c.

It has long been the opinion of the author of this work, that Mr. PITT is either a republican in his principles, or that his intellects are so insufficient, as to prompt him to the furtherance of measures, which seem more beneficial to the advancement of republicanism, than the health of the monarchy; and we hope the error may not be consummate, before the latent poison may have consumed the vitals of loyalty. His movements have been so unnecessarily circuitous; so proverbially imperious; so pitiably cunning; so progressively calamitous; so unfortunate for the nation, and so perilous for his Majesty; that we cannot forbear attaching to him the monkish exclamation, *Quem Deus vult perdere, prius dementat!*—If there are persons who believe that the Minister was exceedingly dispirited and unhappy, at the various inconveniences which the PRINCE endured, and particularly his uneasiness to have his views so egregiously misconstrued, we must regret that the knowledge of the human heart is so imperfect. Few persons have it in their ability to be more thoroughly acquainted with the present state of the metropolitan newspapers than we are; and there is nothing more certain, than that those which are *in the guidance of the Treasury* have been working, for several months, to effect the debasement of the PRINCE of WALES; nor could they, nor would they, be so systematic in their envenomed insolence, or so infuriate in their malice towards the most inconsiderable person in society, were they not *directed*, perhaps *commanded*, to be thus partially and personally undermining and illiberal.

The Public are now in possession of nearly all the evidence relating to this unpleasant occurrence, and which has been hitherto suppressed from the best motives; but as the artifices daily multiplied, and the plot became more important from its duration, it was considered as an act of expediency and honor to tear off the enveloping drapery from all the agents, and present them naked to the contemplation of mankind.

With

With Policy's cameleon host,

Civility's but Friendship's ghost :

Some seem to drive their neighbour on,

Who really wish the dolt undone :

Yet to say P—T abhors the *whigs*

As much as GOLDSMID, MAWBEY's pigs,

Would be absurd as my supposing

Equity 'mid the judges dozing :

Yet now they mingle as they may,

Rare spirits all, *blue, black,* and *grey ;*

Drawing too fast on destiny,

And some (how hapless !) hope to be

Fed like the prophet in the vale,

When ravens brought him cakes and ale ;

With hunger'd cormorants' inclinations,

Grappling at all the good of nations.

Ne'er can my mind forget the view,

When B—— led on the recreant crew :

I'm dizzy when I read his name ;

I shrunk with horror when he came ;

I fainted when I saw him drag

His DOGS to bark at Peace *, and brag

Of

---

* What miserable sensations it excites, to look back on the history of this country (and indeed most others), and observe what few and short intervals of peace a century affords !

To take *our* retrospect no farther back than from the Revolution, which naturally brought a war with it, the account stands as follows:

Of dread achievements, in the womb
Of Time, to glut a kingdom's tomb!

As

In 1689 War commenced.				Years of War.	Years of Peace.
1697, Peace,	—	—	—	8	—
1702, War,	—	—	—	—	5
1713, Peace,	—	—	—	11	—
1718, War,	—	—	—	—	5
1721, Peace,	—	—	—	3	—
1739, War,	—	—	—	—	18
1748, Peace,	—	—	—	9	—
1756, War,	—	—	—	—	8
1763, Peace,	—	—	—	7	—
1775, War,	—	—	—	—	12
1783, Peace,	—	—	—	8	—
1792, War,	—	—	—	—	9
1796, ——	—	—	—	4	—
				50	57

So that out of the last hundred and nine years, we had fifty of open war, besides two Scotch rebellions, and a variety of expensive armaments, little better in some respects than actual war; and yet we have chosen the century most favourable to peace, perhaps, of any in the English history. If it were inquired what advantages have been derived from such frequent, bloody, and expensive conflicts, we know of none, except the enormous increase of the national debt may be reckoned as one, as some people seem most ingeniously to imagine.—Before the present war, this debt was considerably above two hundred and fifty millions: what it may be at the termination of it, heaven only knows! At present Mr. PITT comforts us with the assurance that the existing war has not cost us more than one hundred millions in four years; and these he thinks very *fortunately* expended, in resisting (as he phrases it) the common enemies of all regular governments!—Yet to suppose that one nation can destroy the intellect of another, is supremely preposterous.

There is assuredly no fixing a precise boundary for intemperate spirits, when overheated by success! It is possible that the French, if generally victorious, may, like the Athenians after the battle of *Salamis* with the Persians, become extravagantly absurd, dictating, and ungovernable!—Notwithstanding appearances, I have many doubts whether the French, as a nation, are capable of receiving and being marshalled by republican institutes! To go on from republicanism to monarchy, is a progression agreeable to the nature of things, when it is considered that Luxury is the offspring of Refinement, Refinement the consequence of Experience, and Monarchy the fosterer of both.

To

As gaunt Alecto smil'd at Sin,

Till Nature shudder'd at the grin :

Drest in their tributary charms,

They sold (full dearly) THEIR ALARMS :

All magnifying buoyant fibs,

While loyal slabb'ring stain'd their bibs :

As every *Thing* expectant stood,

And nam'd his price for doing good,

To return from corruption to simplicity in an instant, is a retrograde motion in a realm of which history cannot furnish an example : - if it should be accomplished, it will form the most extraordinary point of wonder, that has occurred from the establishment of society to the present day :—we shall no longer rely upon the influence of habit, but believe the elements of our education may be as readily overthrown as a molehill, and the very attributes and principles of our nature, as changeable as our garments.—Without venturing a sentiment by the way of explanation, it appears to me that the germinating influence of Philosophy, which has in so material a degree weakened the interests of Christianity, has introduced a spirit of disregard for the future, which impels men of all nations, thus actuated, to resign their lives, with an apparent fortitude hitherto unknown within the pale of Christendom ; and if that high impulse which we denominate heroism, is to be ascertained by such a contempt of existence, I fear that neither the pages of the fathers of the church, nor the less rigorous maxims of modern origin, will be equal to the reinstatement of those convenient principles of faith, to which the power is ascribed, of making us blessed independent of action, and happy independent of thought The Greek republicans mingled a noble ardor of piety with their undauntedness; they disdained the warriors of the southern world, because they imagined them impure, voluptuous, and the minions of Venus: their protectress was Juno, who enforced chastity and honor; and they would not admit that *Darius* or *Xerxes* could be comparatively great with men who practised virtue and feared the gods. While the Greek states were shaken with apprehensions from the prodigious armies of Asia, they evinced firmness, unanimity, and rectitude, but no sooner were those fears removed, than Civil Discord brandished the torch among them, and sent her relative Ambition, whose evil suggestions made them harass and exterminate each other !

It was a valuable remark of *Plato*, that nothing was more to be dreaded in a state than the common effect of an excessive liberty.

(I call

(I call them *things*; you smile; what then ?

Will future ages call them men ?)

One ask'd a kingdom as a toy,

The next a pension for his boy;

The third a rattle for his dame,

The fourth a vizor for his shame;

The fifth to be a butcher burn'd,

The sixth to lace that coat he'd turn'd ;

The seventh the car where Neptune rid,

The eighth *good grounds* for what he did * ;

The ninth to mount his wooden guns,

The tenth to eat up *Gallia*'s Huns ;

The eleventh a cap and gilded coach,

And all a passport from REPROACH !

While the good Monarch stood and thought,

Which had *least* worth, who sold or bought.

The bargain seal'd, the claimants blest,

A JESUIT thus the group addrest :—

" Why hang your heads, and blush, and pout ?

You're better surely *in* than *out* :

Who was it mutter'd, as he stood,

'Bout honor and the public good ?

—The public good ! poh, what is that ?

The Public is a beast, that's flat ;

But not of many heads : we'll bawl,

The *Public*'s got—no head at all !

---

* This is evidently an unhandsome allusion to a very noble Duke, who, it is reported, procured from the Crown an immense grant of land, near the metropolis, in consequence of his public renunciation of the political errors of his youth.

When

When Russel bled, IT saw him die
Quiescent—and would you or I,
Or any other *worthy man* :
Then put your *pottage* in your can.
Your worldly sage (thus sophists say)
Can barter grace by either way.
Like turnips on yon acres sown,
You'll thrive the more when trodden down.
Virtue's like doublets made of drugget,
"Twill tear the more, the more you lug it.
Society, in every nation,
Is now but mere sophistication.
That caitiff sure deserves reproof,
Who scuds to heal an ass in's hoof :
As, if he should, 'tis ten to one
He'd kick his teeth out when he'd done :
Thus gnats will fly against a glass,
And buzzing loud demand a pass;
Yet those who put their hands to bring
'Em in the true road, the vermin sting :
And moths you've rescu'd from the flame
(Deaf to or principle or shame),
Steal through the crannies of your chest,
And feed upon your bridal vest.—
God never meant that man should toil
Beneath the surface of the soil,
Or grub 'mong mines on's hands and knees,
To cull repellents to disease,
And cure by Nature's guts and garbage,
What could be better done by herbage.

All

All cooks, who would be paid or priz'd,
Must send their aliment disguis'd.
Faith, like the Poles, has her demesne,
Partition'd by the weak and vain.—
If the world wets you with their spittle,
Give them contempt, 'twill cost you little.
When panting herds *descend* to drink,
And lave 'em in the water's brink,
Myriads of flies rush on to sting 'em,
Anger'd that fate such draughts should bring 'em :
Then does the fierce high-mettled steed
Smite, with his tail, the troublous breed,
Scorning by nobler means than those,
To extirpate the dung-bred foes.—
Touch'd by Pythagorean lights,
Once Fear restrain'd *my* appetites :
And though by varied evils baited,
I scarce could kill the thing I hated :
Ee'n *fleas* approach'd my mental eyes,
As *dancing-masters,* in disguise ;
I swore that *pikes,* though meant to dress,
Were *lawyers'* spirits in distress ;
And that a *toad* had previous been,
In Lewkner's-lane, a child of sin :
A *pack-horse* made my heart quite full
Of grief—I said it was JOHN BULL.
Methought swoln LIVERPOOL a *rat,*
Gnawing the King—JOHN SCOTT a *cat,*

Watching

Watching for *corresponding mice*;
And ADDINGTON a piece of ice:
THURLOW, a tanner's dog, that's sulky;
CURTIS, a whale, with blubber bulky;
Old Q. as Time, contracting weeks;
Sir WATKIN's soul among the leeks!
But now, thank heaven, the film's remov'd,
And here stands MUN, who's self-reprov'd."—
Each having all that he desir'd,
The BAWD to B————d retir'd:
While the remainder took their oaths,
Kiss'd the *King*'s ****, and chang'd their clothes:
    WINDHAM is here, as pleas'd and mild
As JOHN with locusts in the wild;
Bipedal anthora of Fate,
He sucks the poison of the state;
Kills off whole armies in a crack,
And bears vast burdens on his back:
Negative proofs with order trip
In vocal octaves from his lip.
Though now he does whate'er we bid,
He once was Opposition-rid;
But then his lungs were ill employ'd,
Like bells which ring not in a void:
If he wounds Love to give him plasters,
And weaves a bliss from our disasters;
Yet it but argues his address,
Who can at once both bleed and bless.

                                                He

He often dreams of GUY, who meant
To blow up church and parliament;
Smells powder-barrels like a crow,
And plots, and tells the when and how :—
When foul opinions make him warm,
He'll war amid the verbal storm;
And foam and blush, and swear and sweat;
But putrefaction causes heat :
He'll cut a fact in subdivisions,
And shake its tenor by collisions;
He'll *indirectly prove* our rights,
Like scenes illumin'd by side lights;
But that shows genius, taste, and parts;
He scorns Perception's vulgar arts :
Obliquity's of truth the test,
And cross-roads often are the best.
If he's a weakness we can blame,
It is his wondrous fear of *shame!*
Shame's the great tyrant of the mind,
That pains and purifies our kind :
When wights on Error's brink are crawling,
She cramps the thought, and stops their falling;
Yet cruelly to good allures,
As the wench cuts us while she cures.
GEORGE ROSE * and he can draw together,
Up hill in any *dirty weather!*

Each

* This inimitable and disinterested drudge of Government was born
in Perthshire in Scotland, where his father, who was an ecclesiastic and a
nonjuror,

Each brushes filth from PITT's old coats,

And loves the stable for the oats!

Their drafts on Fame (for both have sought her)

Unite their hopes like brick and mortar.

When

nonjuror, maintained a large family with decency and repect, upon an annual income not exceeding sixty pounds; and I must presume, never could expect, in the most flattering among his visions, that his indefatigable son GEORGE would be eventually so elevated by his *merits*, as to become the umpire of a county election—confidential secretary to the Premier— a *distinguished* member of the senate—a Clerk of Parliament—with numerous other appointments, that would crush a man less powerful in mind and body than himself, and which, even with him, might be rendered intolerable, if not sweetened monthly with the inconsiderable remuneration of fifteen hundred guineas!

Mr. ROSE is admitted to be incomparable as a man of business; and I am so thoroughly persuaded this remark is true, that I believe he would have shone with as much splendor behind a haberdasher's counter, as he does in the *sanctum sanctorum* of Downing-street;—he never betrayed a symptom of reflection, though he fattens like a harvest-bug in the hot beam of patronage. He accompanied LORD THURLOW to Paris, a few years since—and a lovely twain they were:—the worthy and accomplished Secretary acted the part of a *receiver-general*; and as he is not too willing to refund, the Ex-chancellor could imprecate and demand without hazarding a reproof from his associate. It must have formed an interesting and novel *coup d'œil*, to have seen EDWARD THURLOW civilly growling at the toilette of MADAME POLIGNAC, and GEORGE ROSE, in the back ground, explaining his hopes and wishes to her *fille de chambre*, through the medium of gesticulation.—When either of them wanted to gratify a passion, they communicated their desires by signs; as, I believe, neither had a sufficient knowledge of the language to have cheapened a pair of pantaloons in the *Fripperie!*

When I visited Warwick Castle, in the year 1792, the porter of the lodge informed me, that a rough black man came to the gate in a summer's evening, and knocked unusually loud: upon his inquiring of the intruder who he was, and what he wanted, by such rude behaviour, the stranger damned him in a tone of thunder, and bid him tell LORD WARWICK that the Chancellor of England desired to see the castle. The menacing deportment of that *sage* and *great* animal so deranged the nervous system of the poor modest

domestic,

When first in office he was brought,

The novel scene o'erthrew his thought ;

He bade his cook *discharge* his wishes,

Fire the peas, and *flank* the dishes ;

Impale the pig, and *flog* the *sutler* ;

Talk'd of *courts-martial* to his butler ;

Drew *plans of war* in spilt champagne ;

Heap'd damson stones as *bodies slain ;*

Re-wrote *dispatches,* in his writing,

And scar'd the women 'bout *bush-fighting ;*

domestic, that he was not perfectly recovered when he communicated the adventure to me.

During a contested election for Westminster, the pure and dignified GEORGE ROSE conceived a sudden and violent partiality for an accommodating publican of the name of SMITH ; and this friendly interference was so ill understood by the people, that a serious inquiry was instituted in the House of Commons ; but the investigation was kindly suppressed, by a nod from the Chancellor of the Exchequer, who very properly thought, that every private transaction was not fit for public discussion !—What can the wise or good utter on the presentment of such a deed, but that their *detestation* for the MASTER, and contempt for *his* MAN, are immeasurable!

As an orator, Mr. ROSE cannot be noted as a diamond of the first water ; for though no person can carry more books under an arm, there are many who carry more of their contents in the head : his powers of ratiocination are materially injured by his bashfulness, and he would be often very luminous, in the path of algebra, if he was less diffident. It has been supposed, that the proximity of his lofty master, on the Treasury Bench, might benumb his faculties ; yet, when I consider his faithfulness and docility, I cannot believe that any would cruelly chill a dependent so meritorious! He has twice endeavoured to rescue his generous principal, in the period of a stormy debate, from the oppressive assaults of Mr. SHERIDAN, by rushing to his defence without being qualified for battle ; but the end never corresponded with the aim ; it was covering the skull of Achilles with a urinal, and not a helmet. Every considerate person must lament the inefficacy of such honest zeal, and especially as he unluckily acquired derision when it was his intention to be useful.

Drew

Drew forth *his pike*, with eyes on fire,

While couchant virgins shun'd his ire !

With other freaks, that seem'd to say

His Wit was sick, or gone astray.

Some madly get a benefit,

Yet know not how to manage it :

As anxious curs, I've heard it said,

Can't find the head or tail o' their bed !

    When I began to pen this letter,

I was, or thought I was, much better.

Alack, alack, I've had my day,

I now must own I feel decay ;

I've borne up stoutly as I cou'd,

But worms will pierce the hardest wood :

They've stole my crutches ; Ruin rot 'em !

They've stopp'd the issue in my bottom :

My hope's defunct—pray what could ail her ?

My eyes are weak, I'll send for TAYLOR.

When in the gripe of death, I'll sing,

Bless the true Church, and SAVE THE KING !

                         Yours, &c.

At the Sign of the World's End,
    Pall Mall,
     Aug. 16, 1796.   JAMES the *Unfortunate.*

P. S. You'll oblige me, dear PAV. when the fish becomes
    cheap,
  To send up a few *maids*, as we've none here will keep.

      END OF THE BRIGHTON GUIDE.

www.ingramcontent.com/pod-product-compliance
Lightning Source LLC
Chambersburg PA
CBHW021514090426
42739CB00007B/607